W9-DHM-647

WITHDRAWN

St. Louis Community College

Library

5801 Wilson Avenue
St. Louis, Missouri 63110

VEGETABLE GARDENING BASICS

VEGETABLE GARDENING BASICS

D. BRUCE JOHNSTONE
ELWOOD H. BRINDLE

Botanical illustrations by
PETER ASCHER, Ph.D.,
University of Minnesota.

BURGESS
PUBLISHING
COMPANY

ACKNOWLEDGMENTS

The authors are particularly grateful to Dr. David W. Davis, Professor of Horticultural Science, University of Minnesota; Dr. James Montelaro, Vegetable Crops Specialist, and Dr. G. J. Stout, Visiting Professor of Vegetable Crops, University of Florida; James Steinert of Cerritos College, California; and Dr. Charles V. Hall, chairman of the Horticulture Department of Iowa State University, for their contributions to the accuracy and completeness of this book. Thanks are also extended to Dr. O. C. Turnquist, Professor, Jane P. McKinnon, Associate Professor, and Shirley T. Munson, Assistant Professor, Department of Horticultural Science, University of Minnesota; June Roget, Librarian, Andersen Library, University of Minnesota Landscape Arboretum; Chase Cornelius, Director of Marketing, and Iver L. Jorgensen, Vegetable Seed Specialist, Northrup, King & Co.

CONTENTS

FOREWORD

People have many different reasons for wanting a vegetable garden. To the majority it's a handy supermarket in the back yard, a bountiful source of appetizing fresh produce. To others it's a fascinating hobby involving creative experiment, discovery and surprise. To some its appeal lies in the deep satisfactions of healthy exercise in the outdoors, coupled with the expectation of solid rewards at the dinner table.

Whatever impels you to plant a vegetable garden, you'll find the experience more productive — and more enjoyable — with a basic understanding of the forces that Nature employs in the miracle of plant growth.

Success or failure in gardening depends on observing certain ground rules that are absolute. If you follow Nature's game plan, you have a reasonably good prospect of harvesting a crop. But failure to observe any one of her rules may lead to decreased yields or even total crop failure.

The knack lies in seeing the big picture at all times, in understanding the interrelationships of sunshine, moisture, soil, nutrients and air that result in the final satisfaction of a full market basket.

Nature's rules have developed over millions of years, as plant life originated in the oceans, gradually crept onto beaches and swamps, adapted to new conditions, and finally developed such tenacious forms that today you can find plants living anywhere on the globe — even under the inhospitable conditions of the polar and desert regions.

Each plant has its own way of surviving, its own set of conditions under which it will thrive. Before we focus in on these individual requirements, we will look at how plants in general develop. Since this field is so vast, our discussion will necessarily touch on only a few basic points. In order to make these points clear, we may occasionally over-simplify. And to hasten reader understanding we may now and then omit what others regard as essential detail. Also, the complexity of Nature is such that exceptions to a good many of our points can doubtless be found by the earnest seeker.

We hope this sampling of the subject will whet a deeper curiosity on your part and perhaps lead to further study in a field that offers limitless potential.

Here, then, are some of the basics of plant development.

NATURE'S GAME PLAN

IN THE BEGINNING, THERE IS THE SEED.

That's how most garden crops start, so that's where we'll begin our discussion of how a vegetable garden comes into being.

A seed is really a neatly packaged plant in miniature. This little miracle of life has been equipped by its parent plant with all of the basic materials needed to produce a mature plant of the identical species and variety, including enough concentrated food to support it until its own food-producing system has been put into operation. It even has a weatherproof coat to protect it while it awaits the signal that conditions are favorable for growth.

WHAT IS THAT SIGNAL?

Actually it's a complex series of signals — notifying the seed that just the right conditions of warmth, moisture and air exist so that it will be safe to begin sinking roots and sending up shoots. But *all* the right conditions have to exist before the seed is triggered into action. Just moisture isn't enough; just warmth isn't enough — the seed has to know that *all* the conditions for successful life are out

there waiting for it: sufficient warmth, the right amount of moisture, the necessary amount of oxygen.

At that point, a fascinating series of events occur:

First of all, the hard covering of the seed coat absorbs water and becomes somewhat soft and wrinkled. Then an embryonic root (called the radicle) emerges from the seed and begins to probe downward. (The root takes a downward path regardless of how the

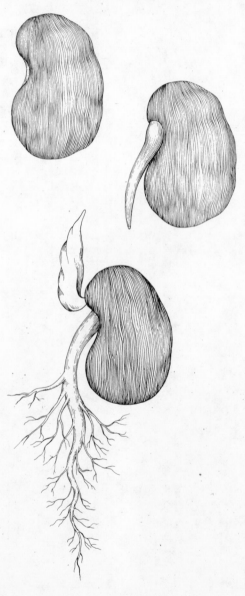

seed is positioned in the soil; it takes
its direction unerringly, guided by a
growth-influencing hormone that is
part of the basic structure of the seed.)
At the opposite end of the seed, the
emerging shoot begins its journey
upwards toward the sunlight, also
guided by hormones. The forces that
control these events are called
"geotropism" and "phototropism."

Meanwhile biochemical forces are at
work stimulating the tiny plant's
growth by softening tissues so they will
more readily absorb water, thus making
the seed's cache of food available to it.
A whole system of roots and root hairs
gradually develops.

ROOTS ARE THE "FORAGERS" FOR THE PLANT

The principal function of roots is to
search out and gather the water-
soluble minerals and nutrients in the
surrounding soil that the plant needs
for growth. Examine a plant root under
a microscope and you will see a
formidable and complicated structure.
Not only does the root have vessels or
tubes to conduct the dissolved
nutrients it gathers; it is also equipped
with storage cells and tiny processing
mechanisms that enable it to maintain
stocks of nutrients until they are
needed by the aboveground part of the
plant.

The probing point of the root is also
specially constructed to enable it to
force its way through and past
obstacles in the soil without damaging
its complex system of pipes and cells.
This is possible because of a protective
shield consisting of scalelike armor
plates that surround the tip of the root.
These plates are constantly being
renewed as they are worn down by
pressure and contact with the rock and
soil particles the root encounters
underground.

Radiating out just behind the rootcap

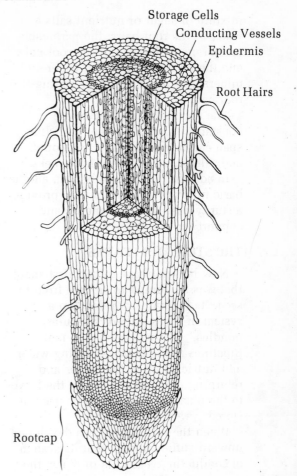

Storage Cells

Conducting Vessels

Epidermis

Root Hairs

Rootcap

are millions of "root hairs." These are
the actual gatherers of minerals and
water, which they absorb through
osmosis and conduct back to the
central root.

The root hairs themselves are
incredibly tiny thin-walled tubes whose
job is to absorb even tinier particles of
water and dissolved mineral nutrients
that can be found in millions of
microscopic openings in the soil. Each
individual particle of soil has dissolved
nutrients adhering to it; the root hairs
line themselves up next to these
nutrients and absorb them by osmosis.
(This is the process by which a strong
solution attracts a weaker solution
through a permeable membrane.)

In this case, the strong solution is the

mixture of sugar or nutrient salts and water in the root hairs; the permeable membrane is the wall of the root hair; and the weaker solution of water and minerals is in the soil surrounding the root hair.

The root hairs themselves are constantly being renewed; their life span can be as little as a few hours, and seldom more than a few weeks.

In addition to food-gathering, another basic function of the root is to provide a sturdy base that will anchor and support the plant.

THE STEM AND LEAVES

Now let's get back to that first shoot that was beginning to emerge from the seed. Its function is to develop a system of tubes, called "vascular bundles," that will act as the main pipelines of the plant, shuttling water and nutrients up to the leaves and returning the food created by the leaves to the places where it is to be used or stored.

When the initial stem has developed upward sufficiently so that its system of conducting vessels is in place, the plant develops its leaves. It is mostly in the leaves that the miracle of photosynthesis takes place.

A "SUGAR FACTORY" IN EACH LEAF

Here is the part of the plant that is vital to the survival of every living thing on earth. Each leaf (or green surface area) contains millions of tiny deposits of a green substance called chlorophyll. When sunlight strikes the leaf, these chlorophyll bodies (or "chloroplasts") effect a combination of water with carbon dioxide, using the sun's energy to form sugar, the basic soluble food upon which all life depends. The water (actually a solution of dissolved nutrients) is piped to the leaf areas from the roots via the network of conductors in the stalk; the carbon dioxide is pulled from the air through tiny openings on the bottom side of the leaf (called "stomata").

In this process of photosynthesis, the molecules of water and carbon dioxide are broken up and reassembled as glucose, or simple sugar. This, in turn, is changed into the building materials

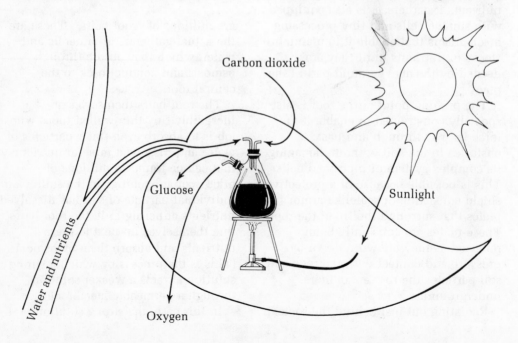

Carbon dioxide

Glucose

Sunlight

Water and nutrients

Oxygen

the plant needs — cellulose, starch, fat, and other carbohydrates. Protein is also manufactured by combining carbohydrates with the minerals those busy roots have been collecting from the soil — nitrogen, phosphorus, potassium, iron, calcium, sulfur, magnesium, etc.

As a byproduct of the photosynthetic process, the leaf also releases oxygen, most of which is vented to the outside air through the same stomata by which the carbon dioxide originally entered.

At this point the plant is fully functioning. The roots are busy collecting moisture and nutrients from the soil; networks of conductors are carrying this material up to the stems and leaves; the products of photosynthesis (sugar, etc.) are being distributed throughout the plant to keep it growing and storing food.

But all this activity takes energy, and where does that energy come from? Originally, of course, it came from the sunlight converted through photosynthesis into simple sugar. The plant gets its energy just as you or I do — by burning up some of this sugar in a process known as "respiration," (which is plant oxidation). This goes on constantly in every living plant. Respiration combines sugar and oxygen to produce energy. At the same time carbon dioxide and water vapor are released by the plant.

During the day, while photosynthesis is taking place, the plant gives out more oxygen than it does carbon dioxide and water vapor. But at night, when photosynthesis is suspended, very little oxygen is produced by the plant and the byproducts of respiration (carbon dioxide and water vapor) continue to be released. For most plants it's important that night temperatures be lower than day temperatures. Respiration speeds up at higher temperature and could use up all the sugar produced during the day. There would then be none left for transfer into cellulose, starch, protein, etc.

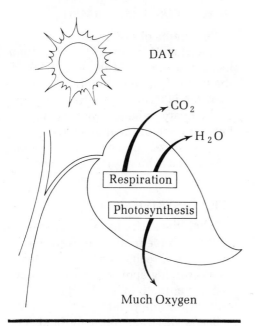

DAY

CO_2

H_2O

Respiration

Photosynthesis

Much Oxygen

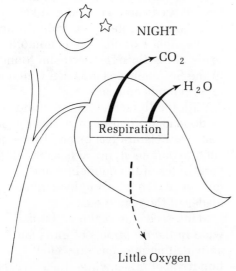

NIGHT

CO_2

H_2O

Respiration

Little Oxygen

FLOWERING

The next big development in the life of most common garden plants is the flowering stage. Nature must provide for the continuation of the species, and flowering is the first step leading toward development of seeds.

Many vegetables flower and produce seed the year they are planted; these are called *annuals*. After producing their seed, this type of plant dies. Other kinds flower and produce seed in their second year, then die; these are called *biennials*. Some continue to flower and produce seed year after year; these are the *perennials*.

Methods of pollination vary, too. Pollination is the transfer of the male sex cells (pollen) of flowering plants to the female part (pistil) of the plant. With some vegetables, such as corn, this is done by the wind. Many tomatoes pollinate themselves, for instance. With others, the job is done by insects or birds.

Let's look at how the latter system works:

Flowers of most vegetable plants contain both basic elements needed for reproduction: pollen-producers (stamens) and ovule-bearing organs (pistils). Since fertilization with pollen from another plant of the same species is normally most desirable, the need is for some way of transferring the pollen.

So again Nature sets up a little factory — this time producing a nectar

that insects like. Glands at the base of the flower exude the nectar; brightly-colored petals with an enticing fragrance advertise the fact that nectar is to be had; insects come to gather the nectar. In order to reach it they must crawl over the stamen and pistils, getting smeared with the sticky pollen in the process. When they move on to the next flower they fertilize it with the pollen they're carrying on their bodies.

HOW SEEDS ARE FORMED

The grains of pollen (the male element) adhere to sticky pads (stigma) located at the top of the long neck of the pistil (female element). Each grain then sends a tiny threadlike tube down to the ovary, where it pierces and fertilizes one of the ovules. Each of these fertilized ovules then develops into a seed which will reproduce the species or variety involved.

SEED DISTRIBUTION

When the seeds have matured, another problem arises in Nature — how are the seeds to be transported to a good growing spot, so that they don't just accumulate in a pile right underneath the plant?

Seeds vary tremendously in size. Orchid seeds are almost dust-like; a single ounce contains several million. At the other extreme, the mammoth seeds of the Coco De Mer palm found in the Seychelles Islands can weigh up to 60 pounds apiece!

With the lighter seeds, the wind can be depended upon to carry them good distances. Nature has given other seeds such ingenious flying aids as the fluffy parachutes of the dandelion and milkweed, the whirling helicopter-type blades of the maple seed.

Many seeds are scattered far and wide in the droppings of birds and animals that may have traveled hundreds of miles while digesting the

fruit or grain whose seed they are now introducing into new territory.

Some seeds are equipped with barbs or sticky substances so that passing animals (including man) will catch them in their fur or clothing and carry them away.

Many water-loving plants (coconut, cattail, lotus) have buoyant seeds so that currents and tides can move them into new areas.

A number of plants have seed pods that literally explode when ripe, shooting seeds in all directions. The jewelweed and wood sorrel are examples.

Some seeds prefer to "travel light." Instead of surrounding themselves with stores of food as other seeds do, they start their life journey in an almost weightless state, relying on the winds to take them someplace where a supply of food exists, ready to nourish them. The super-light orchid seeds we mentioned are of this type.

THE SEQUENCE BEGINS ALL OVER AGAIN

Once the seed finds hospitable soil offering warmth and moisture, the whole cycle repeats itself.

YOU MUST BRING ALL THESE ELEMENTS TOGETHER FOR A SUCCESSFUL GARDEN

Now that you have a basic understanding of how a plant grows, let's examine more closely the factors that control success or failure in a vegetable garden. The first thing we will discuss is

SOIL

The soil we're going to talk about is the thin upper layer of earth containing minute particles of rock, minerals, humus and moisture that overlies the earth in varying depths from a few inches to many feet. In most of this country's inhabited areas the depth of topsoil is sufficient for productive gardening; it can usually be said that any soil that will grow weeds will also grow most vegetables, if managed properly.

Examine your soil closely and you'll find that it has characteristics lying somewhere in between the extremes of clay (which is fine-particled, heavy, and tightly-packed) and sand (larger-particled, gritty, loose-flowing,

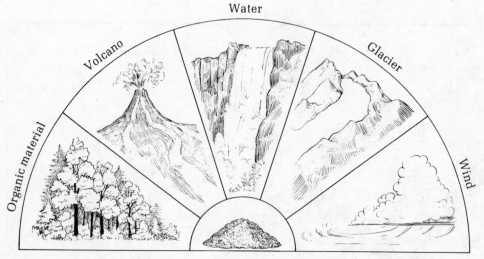

Water

Volcano

Glacier

Organic material

Wind

SOIL

usually light-colored). If you're very lucky, your soil is what is called "loamy" in character — in temperate regions, it's fairly dark, holds moisture well, and is neither too heavy nor too light.

Soil characteristics vary considerably all over the country. The soil in your particular area may have been created by the gradual weathering of rock over the centuries, the grinding action of glaciers, or the eruption of volcanoes. It may have been blown in from other areas by strong winds or carried in by rivers and streams.

Mixed in with the soil are varying amounts of organic material. In desert areas, very little of this is present; in regions of lush growth the soil might have so much organic material that it has the consistency of muck or peat.

WHAT MAKES AN IDEAL SOIL?

To explain this we have to go back to those root hairs which we discussed previously. As we mentioned, root hairs are constantly foraging in the soil, gathering up water and minerals for the use of the plant. The root hairs operate in the spaces between soil particles; this means they can only do their work if there is room for them to maneuver

underground. Also the soil must contain plenty of the needed nutrients plus water and oxygen.

In closely-packed soils there is usually an ample supply of nutrients because that type of soil tends to retain whatever is put into it. But the tiny soil particles are packed so closely together root hairs have a difficult time penetrating between them.

In sandy soils, on the other hand, the root hairs have no trouble penetrating, but the soil structure is so loose that moisture is not retained very long and minerals tend to leach out quickly. As a result, this type of soil usually needs more frequent watering and the addition of extra plant nutrients in the form of fertilizer.

SOIL QUALITY CAN BE ADJUSTED

If Nature hasn't provided you with good, loamy soil there are many things you can do to improve it. The remedy is much the same whether your soil is too heavy (clay) or too light (sandy): Apply liberal amounts of organic matter — barnyard manure, peat or compost. Another method is to sow a cover crop in the fall (winter rye is recommended) to be turned over in the spring.

Clay soil

Sandy soil

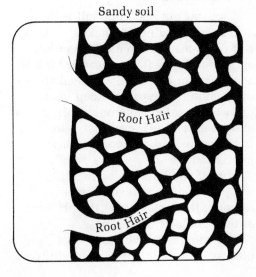

SOIL TESTS

Perhaps you will find that you have soil that is too acid or too alkaline. Either extreme is equally bad for your garden; most vegetables do best on a neutral or slightly acid soil.

In general, most soils in the eastern half of the United States tend to be somewhat acid, those in the western half more alkaline. The soil's level of acidity/alkalinity can be determined by a simple test that establishes where it stands on the pH scale. This is a handy technical measurement ranging from 0 to 14, with the 0-7 end of the scale being acid and the 7-14 end alkaline. The average soil registers between pH 5 and pH 8.

Most commonly grown vegetables are adapted to a somewhat narrower range, between 5.5 and 7.5. If you believe your soil either too acid or too alkaline, it is a good idea to determine its pH rating. This can be done with a testing kit offered in many catalogs, or you may prefer to have your county agent or State Agriculture Experiment Station advise you about the procedure for having a laboratory test made.

HOW TO CORRECT pH DEFICIENCY

If it turns out that your soil is too acid or too alkaline, the next step is to add recommended amounts of either agricultural lime (to correct too high an acid level) or if the soil is too alkaline, either sulfur or gypsum. Keep in mind, however, that too generous applications may result in a pH level that is too far in the opposite direction, which will be just as bad.

Also, if you have added manure, compost or other soil conditioners recently, these may affect the pH level as they gradually decompose.

Correcting a pH deficiency is a slow process; be sure to apply your additives well in advance, preferably the previous season.

HARDPAN

Sometimes the soil may appear to have a good loamy consistency that should result in normal drainage and healthy root development but instead, you find that water tends to stand in pools after a rain, or there is fast run-off; roots stay near the surface and dry out quickly. This may indicate the existence of a layer of hardpan in the soil close to the surface. Hardpan is a cementlike layer of soil that is formed of tightly packed clay particles. Roots find it impossible to penetrate this shield and radiate horizontally in search of water and nutrients. This results in shallow-rooted plants that are unable to survive even short periods of drought.

Hardpan

Hardpan can be detected by probing with a steel rod. When found, it must be broken up with a hammer and chisel or similar equipment. The area covered by hardpan varies considerably; be sure to determine its extent with careful probing.

WATER

Now we come to probably the most familiar — yet often the most misunderstood — factor in successful gardening. Water's importance in Nature's scheme of things goes way back to when plant life started in the oceans. The simple floating algae of those times merely absorbed nutrients from the fluid in which they were constantly bathed. Then more complex plants came into being and gradually established a foothold on land. This required the development of water-seeking roots and circulatory systems so that the plants could get the moisture and nutrients the seas had formerly supplied.

A WATER "BANK" KEEPS PLANTS SUPPLIED

The first primitive land plants were able to survive because their roots found a high water table near the ocean. By sinking roots into this readily available reservoir, they were able to thrive in spite of periods of drought that would otherwise have wiped them out.

In the millions of years that have passed since then, plants have developed many shapes and forms. But this basic requirement still exists — they must have a supply of water that they can tap to keep themselves constantly supplied.

This is why deep watering of vegetable gardens is a necessity. When you soak the soil to a good depth — from eight inches to two feet — plants are able to sink deep, healthy roots. It's far better to water your garden thoroughly and less often than it is to give it frequent short sprinklings.

Generally your garden will require the equivalent of about an inch of water each week by rainfall or irrigation throughout the growing season. In spring and early summer, plants are drawing on water stored in the soil from winter snows and the fall and spring rains. Later on their water needs decrease, and if you're lucky

enough to get a gentle one-inch rainfall each week in the summer you'll have no watering problems. But it is likely that the summer may bring long periods when the sun is blazing hot, drying winds blow, and no rain falls. Then watering becomes crucial to gardening success.

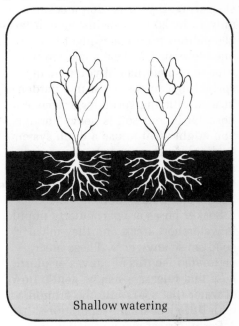

Shallow watering

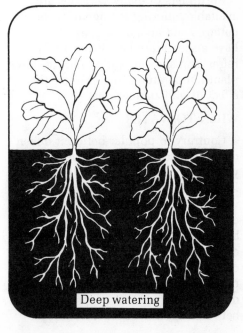

Deep watering

HOW TO WATER

If possible, use some kind of slow continuous-flow watering equipment to lessen the temptation to quit before you've given the soil a good, deep watering. The quantity of water it takes to duplicate natural rainfalls is staggering. If your garden measures only 15 by 20 feet, for instance, it takes 200 gallons from your spigot to equal a one-inch rainfall. That's just too many trips to contemplate if you're using a sprinkling can, so invest in a garden hose, oscillating sprinkler or soaker hose. Or if your soil is heavy enough you might want to use a ditch system — dig deep furrows between rows or sections and fill them with water to create irrigation ditches that will assure deep water penetration.

Soaker hoses are particularly popular in watershort areas, and they make good sense anywhere. These are perforated lengths of canvas or plastic hose that release a steady, gentle flow of water that soaks into the ground with little loss from evaporation.

Sprinklers of many varieties are available, offering a range of watering patterns and area coverages. These have a secondary benefit in that a refreshing shower tends to bring down plant temperatures and counter the effect of midsummer heat.

WHEN TO WATER

Contrary to popular belief, it doesn't matter particularly what time of day you do your watering. Plants are not likely to be damaged by midday watering — the principal disadvantage of watering then is the increased loss by evaporation. As we have pointed out, the plants themselves are constantly venting water vapor which reached them via their roots. Every drop of moisture that evaporates between the time it leaves your sprinkler and the time it reaches those underground roots is lost forever to the plants. Your job is to make sure those roots have an adequate supply of water, whether through natural rainfall or your own efforts.

WATCH OUT FOR WATER "THIEVES"

In any natural surroundings there is constant competition for all available nutrients and soil moisture. Since most vegetable plants are about 90% water and are constantly losing moisture through transpiration, their need for it is particularly serious. And in or near every garden are all kinds of other living things competing for the water you want to reach your vegetables.

Principal among these competitors are trees. A single full-grown tree can use 15 or 20 gallons of water a day, which is quite a large chunk of the normal rainfall available. Tree roots extend out quite a distance — usually as far as the outermost leaves of the tree — and tend to thrive and multiply in a nearby watered garden. Thus it's a good idea to avoid planting your garden in the close vicinity of a tree. (You'll also avoid the shade problems caused by trees.)

Weeds are also big users of the

moisture in your garden. Regular cultivation will keep the weed population down and insure that your crops get the water intended for them.

PERCOLATION RATE
VARIES WITH SOILS

Water percolates down through the ground at different rates, depending on the type of soil you have. In heavy clay soils, water movement is much slower than in sandy soils. Because of the greater colloidal content of clay, water filtering down from the surface takes quite a long time to percolate through. For this reason, clay soils hold water longer and will continue to supply plants with moisture during extended drought periods, while sandy soils will need more frequent irrigation in order to sustain plant life.

Here again we see the continuing interrelationship of soil and water in the growth and development of plants. Full utilization of water calls for a loamy soil that is neither too heavy nor too light. When soil conditions are ideal, water is held by the soil long enough to be absorbed by the root hairs. Heavy clay soil tends to hold it much longer, and this can result in overly moist conditions. This type of soil is also more difficult to work or till. Loose, sandy soil permits too-fast

percolation, with the result that water disappears down into the underlying rock strata before the plants have a chance to use it. Heavier soils such as clays should be mulched.

WHAT HAPPENS WITH
TOO LITTLE WATER

When a plant is deprived of water, a number of events start taking place. The first is a gradual closing down of the stomata pores on the underside of its leaves. As we explained previously, these stomata pull carbon dioxide from the air which is combined with water to form sugar through photosynthesis.

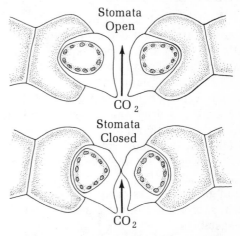

Without a good supply of water, the intake of carbon dioxide must be cut down. At first the plant merely

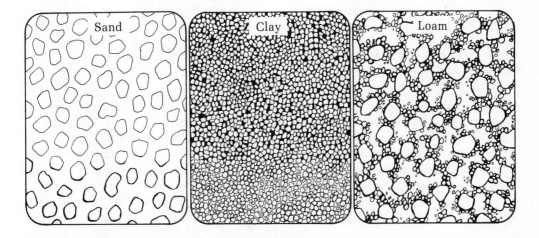

decreases the length of time the stomata are open each day; they may be shut down early in the afternoon, for instance. Production of sugar via the photosynthesic process is cut down accordingly. Plant growth, root and fruit development are all retarded.

If the water supply continues to dwindle, the plant closes up its photosynthesis operation completely, and starts living on its reserve substances. At this point the plant wilts. Continued water deprivation will finally result in the death of the plant.

WHAT HAPPENS WITH TOO MUCH WATER

It's possible to overwater your garden, and under certain conditions it's very easy to do. Too-frequent watering of plants in warm, moist clay soil can cause plants to absorb too much water for their own good. With an active, healthy root system operating in soil packed with moisture and nutrients, the plants actually bulge with excess water and food. Fast, leggy growth takes place; cell walls break, and growth cracks occur on tomato fruits, onion bulbs, carrots and other vegetables.

This condition intensifies when weather conditions inhibit normal transpiration of the plants. Wet weather, high humidity, little air movement can combine to accelerate the development of growth cracks.

OVER-FERTILIZING CAN CAUSE REVERSE WATER FLOW

An interesting sidelight on the absorption of water by plants is the effect that over-fertilizing can have on the osmotic action of root hairs. As we explained previously, these tiny hairs absorb water because they contain a solution of several nutrients and water that is stronger than the water/mineral solution in the surrounding soil.

However, an overly heavy application of fertilizer can reverse this situation — the solution surrounding the root hairs becomes stronger than that within the root walls, and osmosis begins moving water *out of* the root hairs (exosmosis) instead of into them. Thus an over-enthusiastic application of fertilizer can result in stunting plant growth rather than stimulating it, and also cause "burning" or drying of leaf edges.

OXYGEN MUST BE PRESENT

The roots of most vegetable plants require oxygen as well as water. Soil completely saturated with water leaves little space for this needed oxygen. This is why good drainage is a necessity. In fact, if overwatering takes place, or if clay soil prevents the percolation of water down to the sub-strata, plants can actually drown as oxygen is excluded. Such plants as tomatoes and eggplant actually begin to wilt when the soil is saturated with water for more than a day.

TEMPERATURE

Just like people, different species of plants tend to have their own marked preferences regarding the temperatures that surround them while they are working. The work of vegetable plants is photosynthesis and the production of the sugar and starches that go to make up the root, stem, leaf, flower and fruit. Some plants do this best when the nighttime temperatures range somewhere between 45° and 60°F. These are known as *cool season crops*. Others do their best when nighttime temperatures range from 60° to 75°F or so. These are called *warm season crops*.

Typical cool season crops are beets, carrots, chives, onions, lettuce, peas, radishes, parsley, turnips, potatoes and rutabagas.

Warm season crops include beans, cucumbers, melon, squash, tomatoes, eggplant, peppers and others.

PLANT GROWTH VARIES WITH TEMPERATURE CHANGES

Even within a plant's favorite temperature range, its behavior varies as temperatures rise and decline. At lower temperatures the rate of vegetative growth is slowed down and the plant tends to accumulate carbohydrates. At higher temperatures, on the other hand, there is a rapid increase in the rate of vegetative growth and the plant tends to burn up its carbohydrates instead of storing them.

This is why unseasonably hot weather early in the growing season can cause plants to grow too fast too soon, resulting in tall, leggy plants with little or delayed fruit or root development.

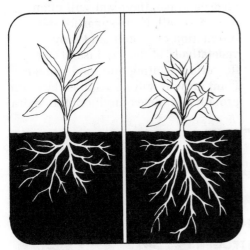

It also explains why the best crops of radishes, peas, beets, lettuce and other cool-season vegetables are produced during the spring and early summer weeks when cool weather encourages slow, steady plant growth combined with maximum storage of carbo-hydrates.

LIGHT

Crucial to the development of any plant is the amount of light it receives from the sun. In the photosynthesis process, light furnishes the energy required to unite carbon dioxide and water to form sugar. The more light that is available, the more carbon dioxide and water the plant can turn into sugar. This means more carbohydrates that can be stored or utilized for plant growth.

Another thing controlled by light is the flowering of the plants. Some will only flower when days are long and nights are short; these are called *long-day* plants. (Radishes, lettuce, beets and spinach are in this category.)

Others flower under short days and long nights. These are the *short-day* plants (sweetpotatoes, lima beans).

Those not influenced appreciably by the day length are called *day-neutral* (tomato, pepper).

Also influenced by light is the time of formation of the underground storage organs of certain plants — potato tubers and onion bulbs, for instance.

This influence of light on plant characteristics, or photoperiodism as it is called, has a great effect on the distribution of both desirable and undesirable plants throughout the country. For example, hay fever sufferers are able to find refuge from ragweed pollen by visiting the far northern parts of the United States. This is because ragweed refuses to flower in any latitude that has more than 14 hours of daylight in the summertime. Thus its optimum growth is confined to a belt roughly south of the 45th parallel.

Photoperiodism is believed to control many other natural events — the migration of birds and fish, the color changes of arctic animals, the fall coloring of trees.

NUTRIENTS

Plant growth and development call for regular supplies of a number of simple compounds, all of which are normally available in the air or soil. We have already discussed two of these: carbon dioxide and water. Among the others are nitrogen, phosphorus, potassium, calcium, sulfur, magnesium, chlorine, iron, manganese, boron, zinc, copper, and molybdenum.

Of these, nitrogen, phosphorus and potassium are "The Big Three" — the most important and most familiar to buyers of commercial fertilizers. The proportions of these elements contained in each bag of fertilizer you buy are expressed in a formula (5-10-5 for instance) that tells you the percentage of each element that the bag contains — nitrogen first, then phosphorus and potassium.

To find out how many *pounds* of each element the bag contains, just take the given figure as a percentage of the total weight of the bag. (Thus a 50-pound bag of 5-10-5 would contain 2½ pounds of nitrogen, 5 pounds of phosphorus, and 2½ pounds of potassium.)

NITROGEN is the main nutrient that must be supplied for the formation of protein by the plant, which is in turn used to create the protoplasm, or living substance of the plant. For this reason, large quantities of nitrogen are needed by the plant while it is growing vegetatively (developing its roots, stems and leaves).

As we pointed out, protein is formed after the photosynthetic process in the leaves has produced sugar. The plant combines this sugar with nitrogen to form proteins, the building blocks of protoplasm.

Given normal amounts of nitrogen, a normal rate of photosynthesis producing normal amounts of sugar, and a normal temperature range, the plant will (a) use up some of the sugar for making protein and (b) store up the rest of the sugar (frequently in the form of starch) in its roots, fruit or seeds.

If too much nitrogen is given to the plant, however, and it is subjected to temperatures in the upper part of its favorite range, the plant will often use nearly all of the sugar for the production of protein and grow vegetatively at the expense of flowering, fruiting and food storage. Plant growth will go wild as the extra protein stimulates production of extra

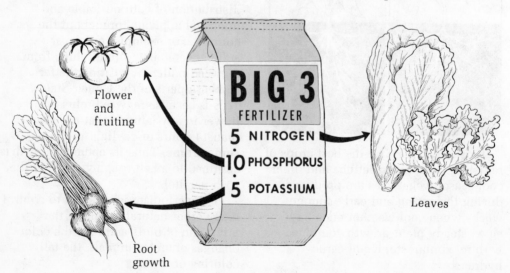

Flower
and
fruiting

BIG 3
FERTILIZER
5 NITROGEN
·
10 PHOSPHORUS
·
5 POTASSIUM

Leaves

Root
growth

protoplasm which forms needless amounts of stalks, leaves, and roots.

This is why it is important to check the formula (5-10-5 or whatever) on every bag of fertilizer you buy. If the proportion of nitrogen is very high, that mixture is not the best one for most vegetable crops and is probably intended more for lawn use, where leaf and stem growth is important for healthy turf. The only types of vegetables on which high-nitrogen fertilizers are usually recommended are leafy crops — Swiss chard, leaf lettuce, celery, spinach, etc. (There are garden fertilizers which contain high proportions of *slow-release* nitrogen. These are acceptable for use on any garden plant.)

A regular supply of nitrogen is required for a healthy garden. It's easy to spot a nitrogen deficiency — the normally deep green of the plants fades to a pale green or even yellow and growth slows down. This is a particular problem in sandy soils.

PHOSPHORUS is required for the formation of starch and some proteins by the plant and is usually necessary for normal flowering and fruit formation. You are seldom likely to give the soil an overdose of phosphorus; little movement or leaching of the compound takes place in the soil.

There are many clues to a phosphorus deficiency: a slowing down of plant growth; little root development; dark grayish-purple leaves and stems; and late flowering and maturing of crops.

POTASSIUM helps reduce nitrates to amino form and is essential to proper development of roots and other underground tissue.

Potassium deficiency makes itself evident in various ways — rough, puckered leaves on potato plants; yellowed edges on cucumber leaves;

retarded development of stems and leaves on tomato plants, along with yellowing of leaves.

Regular applications of the "Big Three" will usually take care of your garden's nutritional needs. Your soil also contains small quantities of the following elements, but deficiencies of these are quite rare:

CALCIUM is vitally necessary for the formation of new plant cells. But its principal function (in the form of agricultural lime) is in controlling the acidity of soils. As we have pointed out, the pH level of soil has a great effect on gardening success. Without considerable amounts of available calcium, many soils would become acid and most vegetables would refuse to grow. On the other hand, too-liberal amounts of calcium would lead to a high alkaline level and equally bad results.

SULFUR helps with both the protein-formation process and the building of cells by the plant. It is acquired both from the air (rain washes it down into the soil) and from deposits in the soil itself. A sulfur deficiency shows up as light green coloring of the veins on leaves that stands out from the normal deeper green of the rest of the leaf surface.

MAGNESIUM plays an important part in the photosynthesis process, since it is necessary for chlorophyll formation. You can spot a magnesium deficiency by the absence of chlorophyll in the tissues between the veins on leaves. The veins themselves will remain green, but the area between them will gradually turn light green and then yellow, starting at the leaf edges and working in.

IRON is also necessary for the formation of chlorophyll, and shows somewhat similar evidence of a deficiency. There appears to be ample iron in the soil over most of the continental United States. In Hawaii, even though the iron content of many of the soils is very high it often is in a chemical form that the plant cannot use, and marked deficiency is seen.

MANGANESE is another element involved with chlorophyll formation. It acts as a catalyst in the process, and a manganese deficiency in plants usually results in less sugar manufacture. A visible symptom is leaves that have a sort of netted appearance with only the veins retaining their deep green color.

BORON (borax or boric acid) is important for tissue development and also aids in plant respiration. Its importance in vegetable crops was discovered only a few decades ago. A boron deficiency shows up in stunted bud development, brittle leaves, woody flesh textures, hollow stems and other conditions. Plants require very small amounts of boron to retain their health, and too-high concentrations can be toxic.

ZINC aids in both chlorophyll manufacture and the process of photosynthesis. A zinc deficiency usually produces abnormally long, narrow leaves which may also turn yellow.

COPPER is vital to the proper functioning of the oxidizing system of plants. A deficiency results in slow plant growth or even a total cessation of growth. Tomatoes planted in copper-poor soil may refuse to flower, and leaves may be curly and bluish-green in color. Copper-deprived beets will have low sugar content.

HOW PLANTS GET NUTRIENTS NATURALLY

The soil may look fairly inert, but actually it teems with life. Billions of tiny organisms live in each cubic foot of soil. Since they can't get energy directly from the sun by means of photosynthesis, they get it by decomposing organic matter around them. (Organic matter is basically any kind of partly or wholly decomposed vegetable or animal matter.)

The organic matter that exists in the soil — whether it was put there by Nature or by humans — is of little value to plants until it has been decomposed. The leaves, weeds, clippings, coffee grounds, manure, sawdust, wood shavings, vegetable trimmings, meat scraps and other organic matter must all undergo decomposition before your vegetable plants will get any benefit from them.

As the micro-organisms go to work on the organic matter they break down the proteins, starches and sugars, releasing heat, carbon dioxide, water,

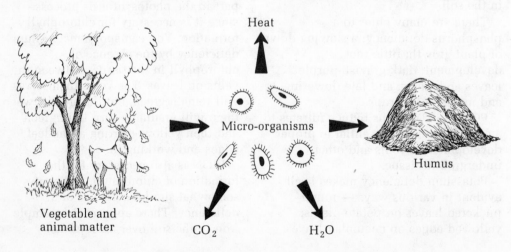

Heat

Micro-organisms

Humus

Vegetable and animal matter

CO_2

H_2O

and other substances including the mineral elements we have just discussed plus inert organic matter that improves soil tilth. Humus, an advanced decomposition product, is composed of extremely fine particles containing a number of chemicals and minerals that have been put into a form that the plants can use. Or, to use the technical term, they have been made "available" to the plants.

When the organic matter has been converted into humus, the root hairs can extract the needed nutrients from the humus and pipe them up to the plant to serve all the purposes we have described — cell formation, photosynthesis, respiration, protein manufacture, reproduction processes, etc.

The humus is extremely porous and each particle can absorb huge quantities of water. This enables it to greatly increase the water-holding capacity of soil. In fact, in equal weights, humus is known to have eight times the water-holding ability of sand and four times that of fine clay soils. What this means, of course, is that soils with high humus content require fewer waterings and can resist drought conditions much better.

Humus or organic matter in soil gives it a more "springy," lively quality. It helps prevent the hardness, compaction and crustiness that highly mineral soils often develop when they're lacking in this material.

ORGANIC GARDENING

There are advantages to both organic and chemical gardening; most gardeners combine some of each. The natural processes we have described are essential to gardening success, and they go on to some extent regardless of how many man-made substitutes a gardener may use for fertilizing, discouraging weeds and dealing with insects. Purists in organic gardening insist on using only natural means to accomplish these ends; chemical gardeners prefer the faster and often more visible results they get with chemical applications, which do not need to undergo decomposition before the plants can use them.

Actually it makes little difference to the plants themselves whether their nutrients come from organic or inorganic sources; they absorb the nutrients in the same manner or chemical form whatever their origin.

The main point of contention between organic and chemical gardeners is the influence of chemicals on the natural balance of life underground and their effect on the nutritional value of crops.

As we have explained, the soil contains countless microbial organisms that are constantly working to improve its fertility through the decomposition of organic matter. Earthworms and many beneficial insects also do their bit in digesting, aerating and enriching the soil. Organic gardeners maintain that the introduction of harsh chemical treatments destroys many of the natural helpers that exist underground and also affects the edibility of crops.

There is evidence that sustained practice of organic gardening methods will strengthen plant life to the point where it may be more resistant to insects and disease. There are also many natural weapons used by organic gardeners. Some import insect parasites and natural predators to keep undesirable insect populations under control; others accept the use of bug killers such as pyrethrum and rotenone since they are organic in origin.

THE COMPOST HEAP

Both organic and chemical gardeners agree that one of the most useful tools

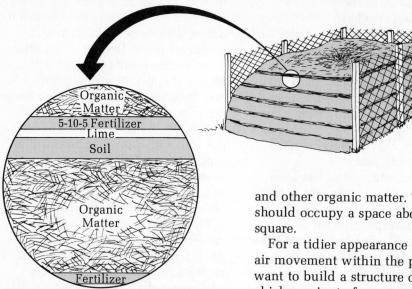

of a gardener is a well-handled compost heap. In effect, this is a planned "humus factory" in which the normal breakdown of organic matter is accelerated. A compost heap also simplifies disposal of leaves and garden trash without the air pollution that results from burning or the inconvenience of bagging and transporting this material to a disposal area.

As we have explained, the organisms that exist in the soil are ready to spring into action the moment any organic matter reaches them. Their job is to oxidize it or reduce it to valuable humus. The compost heap is designed to provide ideal surroundings for these organisms, supplying a maximum of the natural helps they need to do the best possible job in the shortest time.

BUILDING THE PILE

This can be as simple or as laborious a procedure as you wish. In its most basic form, a compost heap is simply an area you mark off in an out-of-the-way section of your garden where you can pile your dead leaves, garden refuse, lawn clippings, weeds and other organic matter. The pile should occupy a space about six feet square.

For a tidier appearance and greater air movement within the pile, you may want to build a structure of boards and chicken wire to form an enclosure for the heap.

Each layer of material you lay down should be about six or eight inches deep. Cover this with an inch or so of garden soil. Then sprinkle on a handful of lime and add a pound of your garden fertilizer, preferably a 5-10-5 formula. Keep adding new layers until the pile is several feet high, watering each layer as it is applied. Keep the material compacted — if it is too loose it will not decompose readily. (Ordinarily building of the pile continues through the spring, summer and fall — whenever organic matter is available.) If you have no easily available source of garden soil to use on the pile, you may want to dig a shallow pit in which to start the pile. Then you'll have a freshly dug mound of dirt you can use for soil layers. But don't dig the pit more than a few inches deep; adequate air circulation is essential for good results.

The top layer of the pile should have a shallow depression in the middle. This will cause rainwater to accumulate and gradually soak into the pile rather than running off at the edges.

Now let's review what we have

accomplished so far in building our compost heap and what is going to happen next.

First of all, we have brought together a number of materials that should decompose quite rapidly. Only organic matter belongs on the pile, of course — no stones or metal or plastic. And the organic matter itself should be of the kind that will rot easily — no large twigs, bones, fat, paper cartons or other items with a slow disintegration rate. If possible, chop up such things as cornstalks, brush, large weeds, tree trimmings, etc., before adding them to the pile. As a general rule, anything more than ¼'' thick will probably take too long to decompose; best results are had when the compost consists mostly of leaves, lawn clippings, hay, manure from farm or domestic animals, sawdust, reject or spoiled garden produce, hedge trimmings, birdcage cleanings, coffee grounds, fireplace ashes, fish scraps, wood shavings, and similar material.

In order to accelerate the natural decomposition of the pile, we have provided all the elements needed by the micro-organisms that will do the work:

NITROGEN, which is used by the organisms in great quantities, is supplied in the fertilizer we added, the manures, the fish scraps, and other nitrogen-rich materials on the pile.

MOISTURE is crucial to the success of your compost heap. Dry materials take forever to decompose; be sure the pile is kept fairly moist at all times. But don't overwater it; if pore spaces in the material are full of water the soil organisms will be deprived of the oxygen they need and decomposition will be slowed.

HEAT is generated as the bacterial action begins, and it increases until the pile has a temperature that can go as high as 160°F. or more. The rate of decomposition gets faster as the pile gets hotter. In fact, it theoretically doubles with every 18°F. rise in temperature. These high temperatures eliminate most of the offensive odors

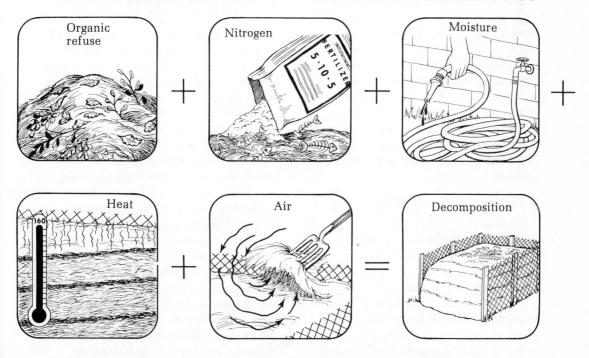

Organic refuse + Nitrogen + Moisture +

Heat + Air = Decomposition

that would otherwise accompany decomposition. They also tend to kill harmful insects and weed seeds that may be lodged in the pile.

AIR is the other vital ingredient of successful composting. Twice each year you should turn over the pile with a pitchfork or spade. Early spring and fall are the best times to do this. Be sure to turn the outer parts of the heap toward the inside so that they will be exposed to the high temperatures at the center of the pile.

Decomposition will take place, but at a slower rate, if too little air reaches the pile. This is because there are two types of micro-organisms at work: the air-loving type (aerobic), which are the most efficient workers, and the anaerobic type, which can operate under virtually airless conditions but are slower to get the job done.

The rate of decomposition is also affected by the climate of your area. Total decomposition can take place in as little as a few months in warm areas; in colder climates it could take years.

If your compost pile has been built correctly, you will usually begin to see results in just a few weeks. The heap will start to heat up and shrink in size. The particles of matter will gradually get smaller and turn darker in color until they are dark brown or even black. At that point the rotted compost (or humus) crumbles easily in your hand and is ready to be applied to your garden.

WHERE TO USE COMPOST

WORKED INTO THE SOIL, well-rotted compost has no equal. It is full of nutrients, has matchless water-holding ability and sufficient bulk to help aerate the soil.

AS A MULCH, compost will do a fine job of keeping down weeds and holding moisture in the soil.

AS SEED-STARTING SOIL, mulch is not only a fine starting medium but it also makes additional fertilizing unnecessary in most cases.

COVER CROPS

While the compost heap is the most common as well as the cheapest source of soil-enriching matter for the home gardener, many people plant ryegrass or vetch in their gardens as soon as possible after the fall harvest. This cover crop, as it is called, serves a variety of purposes. As it takes root in the fall, it protects the soil from erosion by wind and rain. It helps to bring leached-out soil nutrients back up to where they will be put to good use. Finally, and most important, when the crop is plowed or spaded under in the spring it gives the soil valuable amounts of nutrients and organic matter. In fact, it is estimated that the nutrients supplied to the soil by a well-fertilized cover crop are equivalent to a ton of fertilizer per acre.

HYBRID VARIETIES

Some of the vegetable varieties you find in seed racks or in catalogs are designated as "Hybrids," which means the seed is a direct cross of two specially-selected parent strains. Hybridization is the result of scientific breeding techniques that search out specific qualities — disease resistance, early maturity, strong stalks, for example — and then combine these qualities in a single variety.

The first efforts at hybridization occurred early in this century when breeding experiments were tried on corn, based on Mendelian laws of heredity. Corn was selected for the initial experiments because its tassel (male part) and silk (female part) are easy to manipulate. Although early results were discouraging, successful crosses were finally achieved and hybrid corn varieties appeared on the market in the early 20's.

Since then many other vegetables have been hybridized, including cabbage, broccoli, brussels sprouts, tomatoes, peppers, summer squash, cantaloupe, watermelon, onions, spinach, turnip and eggplant.

The process of developing a hybrid is a fascinating one. Basically all plant species, varieties and cultivars have individual differences that distinguish them from other species, varieties and cultivars. But going a step beyond this, even the individual plants within each group have minor differences that scientific plantsmen can spot. Or to use the scientific term, the plants are *heterozygous.*

By inbreeding (self-pollinating) in the same plant over many generations, these minor character differences are brought out in many *lines* or *races* of the original species, variety or cultivar. Each line becomes extremely uniform (*homozygous*) and a marked decrease occurs in both size and vigor.

But when certain of these "pure" lines are crossed, hybrids are produced that almost always show a dramatic increase in vigor, size and yield over the original species, variety or cultivar. This is called *heterosis.*

If the final cross (after the hundreds of preliminary experimental crosses)

includes parental characteristics that complement one another, not only do vigor, size and yield increase, but there are also desirable changes in color, maturity, disease resistance, etc.

For commercial growers, the aim of vegetable breeding is to find strains that not only have high yields and few disease or insect problems, but also offer qualities that will make the harvesting, shipping and selling of the produce easier. This means uniform maturities (so that harvesting schedules can be set up and met); uniform sizes (whole tomatoes that fit the can exactly, for instance); skins that don't bruise easily (to survive the rugged journey to market); and the ability to retain fresh good looks on the supermarket shelves for an extended period. Vegetables with these qualities also permit mechanical harvesting, including the "once-over" system in which machines move through a field, harvesting the crop and destroying the plants in one sweep.

Hybrid seeds cost a bit more because of the extra work that is involved in producing them (each generation must be directly crossed under controlled conditions). But in return, you can usually expect better quality, unique color or flavor, and a higher yield coupled in some cases with better disease resistance.

STEPS
TO
SUCCESSFUL
GARDENING

PLANNING THE GARDEN

As with any undertaking, the first step in gardening is to think about what you want to accomplish and how you propose to do it. The best way to start your planning is to sit down with a pencil and paper. Lots of paper — once you start putting possible garden arrangements down, you'll find that the ideas come thick and fast.

A word of caution, however — it's easy to get carried away when you're jotting down diagrams. Be sure to keep certain realities in mind, such as:

WHO'S GOING TO DO THE WORK? Will your garden be a whole-family project with plenty of willing hands available throughout the growing season, or will you be the only participant — in between golf and tennis, that is?

WHAT VEGETABLES DOES YOUR FAMILY LIKE TO EAT? A home garden makes it possible to indulge individual tastes to a great extent. Besides giving extra space to favorite vegetables, you can plan successive plantings and intercroppings to increase yields. Be sure your garden plan reflects definite preferences and is not just a series of arbitrary space allotments. You'll probably want only a few plants of parsley or chives, for instance, and long rows of carrots, beets or onions.

HOW MUCH AVAILABLE SPACE? By this we mean usable garden area — not just empty ground. There is a big difference, as we will explain later.

DO YOU PLAN TO CAN, FREEZE OR STORE YOUR HARVEST? This is a factor both in planning your garden and in choosing the varieties you plant. Keeping qualities vary considerably; you might want to get advice on this from friends who do a lot of vegetable preserving. In any event, choose seeds carefully; make sure the kinds and varieties you plant are adapted to your area, climate, and growing season. Generally the seeds available at your local garden center or supermarket have been selected for their suitability to local conditions. Most seed companies vary the contents of their seed racks geographically, stocking them with varieties most likely to be successful in a given area. In ordering from seed catalogs, keep in mind any weather characteristics of your area that may affect seed performance.

CHOOSING THE SITE

The first consideration in locating your garden is finding a sunny spot. It's possible to make up any other

Avoid shaded locations; your garden needs a minimum of six hours of direct sunlight daily.

deficiencies a site may have —
moisture, nutrients, air, etc. — but if
you plant your garden in a shady spot
there's absolutely no way you can
provide a practical substitute for that
all-important sunshine. Besides
creating the miracle of photosynthesis,
sunshine powers all the other activities
of plant life. *At the very minimum, the
spot you choose should have six hours
of sun a day.*

Pick a spot not too close to buildings,
fences, hedges and walls. (It's a good
idea to check your possible sites
occasionally throughout a full day —

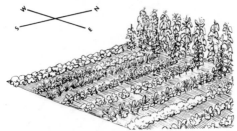

**Place tall plants at north end of garden to
avoid shading others.**

shadows can be surprisingly long.) And
most important — keep as far away
from trees or shrubs as possible. Not
only do they cast unwanted shade, but
their roots are constantly on the prowl
for new sources of moisture and
nutrients.

The site you choose should be fairly
level and well-drained. If it has a slight
slope, that's fine. But if the land drops
more than one foot in 50 feet or so,
you're likely to have erosion problems.
In that case, run your rows across the
slope or form contour terraces. This
will tend to minimize washing during
heavy rains.

If erosion is no problem, it's a good
idea to run rows north and south, so
that each row receives an equal amount
of sunlight.

HOW MUCH SPACE?

In figuring the amount of space you
have available, remember that no law
says your garden must occupy a neat
rectangular space at one end of your
property. If your sunniest, most
desirable spots are at the edge of
driveways or patios or are now
occupied by flower borders or strips of
lawn, consider using these areas for

vegetable plantings. These offbeat locations offer many advantages you might not have thought of: they're usually closer to the house and therefore more convenient for watering, cultivating and harvesting; you can more easily spot wilting or signs of insect invasion in time to correct them.

MIX FLOWERS AND VEGETABLES IF YOU WISH

Many gardeners plant a few vegetables in with their flowers, and the visual results can be stunning. The interesting shapes and textures offered by loose-leaf lettuce, chard, kale, endive, parsley, or peppers blend well with most flowers, and such vegetables as eggplant and chives produce delicately tinted blossoms as well.

GARDEN AWAY FROM HOME

If adequate space isn't available on your own property, you should consider renting garden space from a neighbor, joining a community garden project or inquiring about odd plots that are sometimes available from highway departments, railroads, airport commissions or other agencies with large real estate holdings.

Once you've decided on where to place your garden, you're ready to consider the size you want. Here is a suggested layout for a small (300 sq. ft.) garden that can produce a goodly quantity of 14 popular vegetables for

1. Pole Beans (⅔ Row on trellis)
2. Cucumbers (⅓ Row on trellis)
3. Tomatoes (6 Plants)
4. Bush Summer Squash (Zucchini) (3 Plants)
5. Bell Peppers (6 Plants)
6. Chard (⅓ Row)
7. Parsley (3 Plants)
8. Chives (3 Plants)
9. Carrots (1 Row)
10. Beets (1 Row)
11. Onions (½ Row)
12. Lettuce (½ Row)
13. Broccoli (½ Row)
14. Radishes (½ Row)

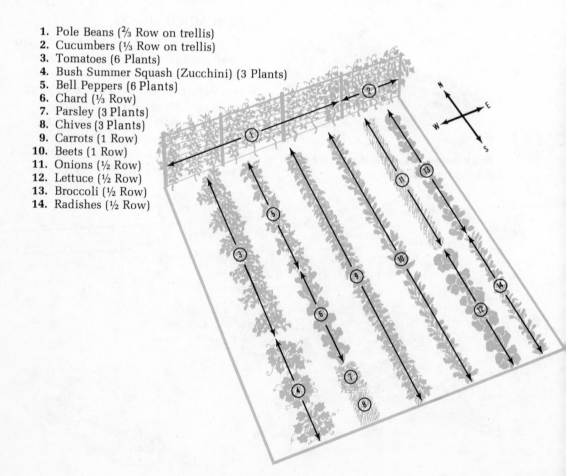

you. Note that the fence or trellis should be located at the north end of the plot so as not to shade the rest of the garden.

If you have the space, a garden measuring about 25x30' (750 sq. ft.) will allow you to grow more tomatoes, beans and cucumbers and perhaps add cabbage, eggplant and potatoes. This medium-size garden should produce enough surplus to permit some canning and freezing.

For a large family, consider going to a plot of about 40x50' (2,000 sq. ft.). This will enable you to plant some of the "space-hogs" — corn, melons, winter squash — along with more of the freezing and canning vegetables (tomatoes, cucumbers, beans, peas, spinach, broccoli, peppers) and quantities of those that store well over the winter (carrots, beets, onions).

SPACE-STRETCHERS

There are a number of ways you can increase the usable space in your garden:

KEEP WALKWAYS DOWN TO A MINIMUM. In a very small garden, paths between rows are often unnecessary; careful planning of rows in larger gardens can eliminate much wasted area. A basic consideration, of course, is whether you plan to use mechanized equipment such as power cultivators. In that case, you will have to plan on enough space between rows for the equipment to move through.

SUCCESSION PLANTINGS save space and also allow a longer series of harvests. Lettuce, peas, radishes, beets, carrots, kohlrabi, spinach, turnips and Chinese cabbage mature early enough so that after they're harvested you can use the same space for another planting of the same or a different fast-growing vegetable.

Oversized walkways occupy valuable growing space and can waste fertilizer and water. Make paths very narrow for hand cultivation, machine width for power cultivation.

INTERCROPPING should also be considered in planning your garden. This is simply mixing different crops together either by alternate planting within a row or squeezing in between rows. The theory of intercropping is to mix slow-growers and fast-growers so that the speedy vegetable has matured before the slower one needs the growing space. This system lets you, in effect, raise two crops in the same space without crowding either.

STAGGERED PLANTINGS will give you more plants in a given area without decreasing the space between plants. Here's how it works. Normally you space plants in even rows like this:

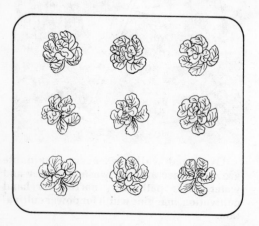

If you stagger the plants, each plant will be just as far from its nearest neighbor, but you have saved considerable row space:

VERTICAL PLANTING is another space-saver. Fences, trellises, stakes and poles let you extend your garden upwards without adding to the soil area. Many crops such as peas and pole beans are strong natural climbers. Others, such as cucumbers, melons and squash will climb if helped and tied.

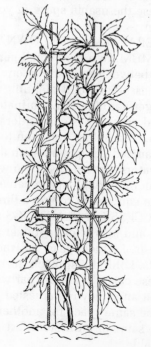

Still others, such as tomatoes, don't climb naturally but do very well at using vertical space if they are trellised.

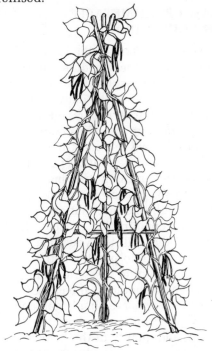

SEPARATE PERENNIALS AND ANNUALS

Most vegetables are annuals — they are planted and harvested each year. A few are perennials — once they are established, they will continue to come up year after year. Among these are asparagus, horseradish, rhubarb and chives. Be sure to allot a separate part of your garden to the perennials (such as a strip along one side), since they will get different treatment from the others and the area they occupy will not be plowed or spaded up each year.

KEEP TALL CROPS IN BACKGROUND

Tall plants such as sweet corn and pole beans tend to shade the low-growers, so it's usually a good idea to place them at the northern end of the garden. Their shadows will then fall outside the garden area. However, some leafy crops like lettuce will tolerate considerable shade.

Another good idea is to plant vine crops (squash, cucumber, melons) at the edge of your garden. These tend to sprawl out quite a bit, and a side location lets them spill over into other areas rather than crowding the garden proper.

WHAT TO PLANT

Family preferences should decide which crops to plant, and how much of each. Keep in mind that some crops keep producing throughout the growing season — tomatoes, broccoli, kale, parsley, snap beans, summer squash, eggplant, peppers, and chard. Others have a short harvest period — peas, radishes and spinach, for example.

Also to be considered is the amount of space each kind of vegetable takes up. Sometimes there just isn't enough room to plant favorites like corn, melons, winter squash or pumpkin, which require lots of space. In that case you're better off planting crops that occupy a much smaller area: carrots, beets, onions, snap beans, lettuce, etc.

If you intend to can or freeze some of the harvest, that can have a big effect on both the size of your garden and the kind of vegetables you decide to grow. Again, by selecting continuous bearers and planning successive plantings you can not only increase yields but also spread the harvest out over a longer period. Many gardeners can or freeze their produce in small amounts over the harvest season. Besides making the work easier, this enables them to capture the peak of flavor.

WARM-SEASON VS. COOL-SEASON VEGETABLES

As we discussed previously, some vegetables like warm weather and others thrive when it's cool. Be sure to allot separate areas for these two types of crops; don't plant the entire garden at one time. This simplifies preparation of the soil bed, since you can work on the cool-season crops early in the season and postpone preparing the rest of the plot until later if you wish.

USING SHADY AREAS

If part of your garden is shaded by trees or buildings for some of the day, be sure to use that portion for your leaf crops, such as lettuce, kale, chard, chives, kohlrabi, spinach, mustard or endive. The edible part of most of these crops is their leafy foliage, and these plants require less sunshine than do vegetables that must develop edible roots or fruit.

CHECK OVER YOUR FINAL GARDEN DIAGRAM

When you have arrived at a garden arrangement that fits all your requirements, check it over once more with these factors in mind:

(1) Does it match the physical area available to you?

(2) Does it include as many of your favorite vegetables as possible?

(3) Have you allotted space wisely, based on the length of crop harvests, the growing characteristics of the plants, the climate in your area?

(4) Have you planned fences and other supports to extend garden space?

DRAW UP A TIMETABLE FOR YOUR GARDEN

Just as important as the layout of the garden is the time schedule you should follow for best results. The basic guide for this schedule is the date the last killing spring frost occurs, on the average, in your area. (See map.)

From this, we can construct a chart of planting and harvesting periods that reflects the particular growing requirements of each vegetable.

Now, with this information, put together a combination timetable and notebook that will tell you what, when and how much to plant, whether transplants should be started and when. There should also be space to enter the date harvesting began and ended, plus comments about the amount and quality of the harvest; insect and disease conditions noted; remedies applied, etc.

On a year-to-year basis this notebook will become increasingly valuable to you. Besides chronicling your garden's performance each year, it will provide useful guidelines for future planning, help you avoid mistakes and let you compare the results you obtain with different varieties.

If the only garden site you have is partially shaded, plant leafy vegetables in the shaded area.

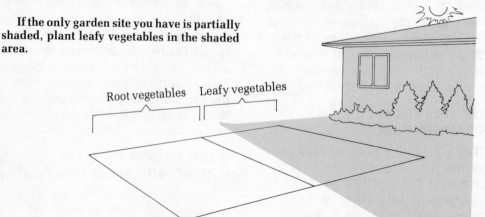

Root vegetables   Leafy vegetables

PLANTING TIMETABLE FOR VEGETABLES

These recommendations are based on U. S. Department of Agriculture
records of average dates of the last killing frost in spring.
Individual conditions may vary, of course.

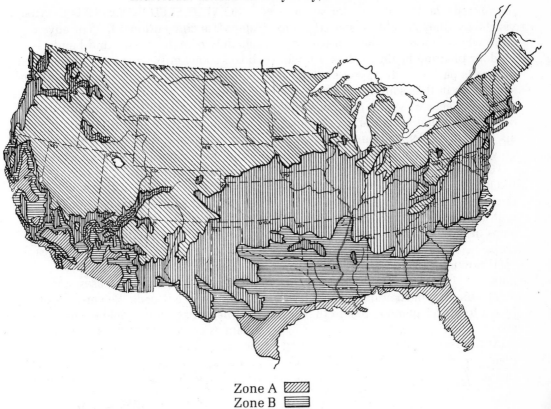

Zone A
Zone B
Zone C
Zone D

	Page	Zone A	Zone B	Zone C	Zone D
Artichoke	120	Feb.-Mar.	Mar.-May	....	....
Asparagus	120	Mar.-Apr.	Mar.-Apr.	Mar.-May	Apr.-June
Beans	66	Apr.-Aug.	Apr.-June	May-June	May-June
Beets	68	Jan.-Dec.	Feb.-Oct.	Mar.-July	Apr.-July
Broccoli	70	July-Oct.	Feb.-Mar.	Mar.-Apr.	Mar.-Apr.*
Brussels sprouts	72	Feb.-May	Feb.-Apr.	Mar.-Apr.*	Mar.-Apr.*
Cabbage	121	Jan.-Mar.	Jan.-Apr.	Mar.-May	Mar.-May*
Carrots	74	Jan.-Dec.	Jan.-Mar.	Mar.-June	Apr.-June
Celery	76	Mar.-June	Mar.-May	Apr.-June	Mar.-June
Chard	78	Jan.-Dec.	Feb.-Sept.	Mar.-Aug.	Apr.-July
Collards	122	Jan.-May	Feb.-May	Mar.-June	Apr.-June
Corn	80	Apr.-June	Mar.-June	May-July	May-July
Cucumbers	82	Apr.-June	Apr.-June	Apr.-June	May-June
Eggplant	84	Feb.-Mar.	Feb.-Apr.	Mar.-May*	Apr.-May*
Endive	122	July-Sept.	Aug.-Sept.	Mar.-May	Apr.-June
Kale	86	Feb.-June	Feb.-May	Mar.-May	May-June
Kohlrabi	123	Mar.-June	Mar.-May	Apr.-May	May-June
Leek	123	Mar.-Apr.	Mar.-May	Apr.-May	Apr.-May
Lettuce	88	Jan.-Dec.	Aug.-May	Mar.-June	Apr.-June

	Page	Zone A	Zone B	Zone C	Zone D
Muskmelon	90	Apr.-June	Apr.-June	Apr.-June	May-June
Mustard	92	Feb.-May	Feb.-May	Mar.-June	May-July
Okra	94	Apr.-June	Apr.-June	Apr.-June	May-June*
Onions	96	Dec.-Mar.	Dec.-Apr.	Feb.-May	Mar.-June
Parsley	123	Jan.-Dec.	Jan.-June	Feb.-June	Mar.-June
Parsnips	98	Mar.-June	Feb.-June	Apr.-June	May-June
Peas	100	Jan.-May	Jan.-Apr.	Feb.-May	Mar.-June
Peppers	102	Feb.-Mar.	Feb.-Apr.	Mar.-May*	Mar.-May*
Potatoes	104	Jan.-Dec.	Jan.-Mar.	Mar.-June	Apr.-June
Pumpkin	124	Apr.-June	Apr.-June	Apr.-June	May-June
Radishes	106	Jan.-Dec.	Feb.-Oct.	Mar.-Aug.	Apr.-July
Rhubarb	108	Feb.-May	Feb.-May	Mar.-May	Apr.-June
Rutabagas	124	July-Sept.	July-Sept.	July-Aug.	July-Aug.
Spinach	125	Jan.-Dec.	Feb.-Oct.	Mar.-Sept.	Apr.-Aug.
Squash	110	Apr.-June	Apr.-June	Apr.-June	May-June
Tomatoes	112	Jan.-Mar.	Feb.-Mar.	Mar.-May*	Mar.-May*
Turnips	116	Feb.-Mar.	Jan.-Mar.	Feb.-Apr.	Mar.-May
Watermelon	118	Apr.-June	Apr.-June	Apr.-June	May-June

*Transplants recommended.

TRANSPLANTS

If the climate in your area makes the use of transplants advisable for some vegetables, they should be started six to eight weeks before the date on which outdoor planting begins. (Thus if frost danger is past on May 1, you should start seeds in flats sometime during the first two weeks of March.) Consult your outdoor planting schedule, work back six to eight weeks, and enter the date on which transplants should be seeded.

TOMATOES, EGGPLANT, PEPPERS, BROCCOLI, AND CABBAGE are the vegetables most often raised with transplants. There are four basic steps in growing transplants of these crops:

(1) Sowing seed indoors in boxes or pots.

(2) Thinning or moving the tiny plants to bigger planters before they get too crowded.

(3) Gradually accustoming the young plants to the outdoors (or "hardening" them).

(4) Setting the plants out in the garden when it's safe to do so.

Let's look at each of these operations in detail.

SOWING SEED INDOORS is the first step. Use conventional flats or any shallow containers you find handy — boxes, pots, milk cartons, cans, etc. Just be sure they have drainage holes at the bottom.

Fill the flats with good quality soil or artificial media — about ⅓ each of peat or humus, garden soil, and some kind of soil conditioner such as sand, vermiculite or perlite.

NOTE: Sterilizing of this small quantity of soil is quite easy, and it can pay big dividends. Just put it in the oven at 180° for a half-hour or so. This kills any harmful organisms in the soil to prevent the development of damping-off or other diseases, and it also kills weed seeds. Be careful not to overheat it as undesirable chemical changes can occur. Let the soil cool before you put it in your flats.

Put several inches of soil in each flat. Do not add fertilizer; this often causes

Tamp down soil in flats with a small piece of wood to create a uniform surface.

too-fast growth in the initial stages and the plants become tall and spindly.

Water the flats well and allow them to drain for a couple of hours before planting your seeds.

Scatter seed about ¼" deep (or twice the smallest diameter of the seed) in rows 2 or 3 inches apart. Gently firm the soil over the seeds. Then cover each flat with sheet plastic or a piece of glass to retain surface moisture. Place the flats in a warm place — between 70° and 80° is ideal. It isn't necessary to keep them in total darkness; just somewhere out of the sunlight.

Insert small labeling stakes in each flat or row so that you can identify the plants easily.

Water the flats only when the soil surface becomes dry to the touch. Resist the temptation to overwater; this can do more harm than good, as we have explained. Usually if glass or plastic is used to cover the watered flat no further watering is necessary until after germination. When the seedlings appear, remove the plastic or glass covering and move the flat to a window to increase daytime light intensity.

THINNING

As soon as the seedlings are 1" high, thin them down or move them to a bigger planter where they'll be 1" or so apart. Since this is the first time the plants will be moved, it should be done carefully. Cut a generous amount of soil out with each little plant as you move it to the bigger container, and water it immediately. If it's necessary to handle the plants themselves, grasp them by their leaves rather than the stems, which are quite brittle at this point.

Keep the flats close to a window, preferably in a somewhat cooler room, where they will get full sunlight. This will have the effect of slowing down top growth and encouraging the plants to develop strong, healthy root systems.

Water the tiny plants regularly, but avoid sprinkling directly on their leaves; this could encourage plant diseases.

When the plants are about 2" tall, it's a good idea to provide them with still more growing room — individual pots or larger flats where they will have about 3" of space between them and their nearest neighbors.

HARDENING

About a week before outdoor planting time, cut back on watering and start exposing the plants to a few hours of outdoor weather each day. This will prepare them for the transition from indoor life to outdoor life and also lessen the shock of physical transplantation, which can be quite damaging.

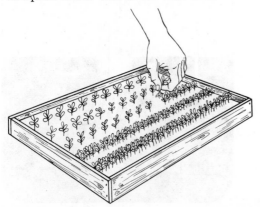

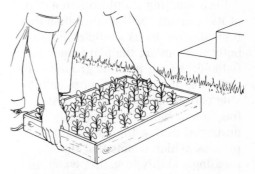

Place flats outdoors for short periods to harden seedlings.

Keep an eye on the plants when they're outdoors during this hardening period. Windy weather can dry them out surprisingly fast. And keep them out of direct sunlight at first; tender leaves will dry out and can burn easily.

SETTING PLANTS OUT

When all danger of frost is past, move the plants outdoors permanently. It's best to wait for a cloudy or rainy day to do this; new seedlings can dry up and die unbelievably fast when it's hot and dry. In fact, if the weather turns clear and sunny for the seedlings' first few days in the outdoors, you should shade them from the sun with any kind of makeshift protection — cloth, slats, upended baskets or whatever.

Move quickly and gently in setting plants outdoors.

Each seedling should retain a clump of its "nursery" soil around it as it is transplanted. Be as gentle as possible both in removing the plant from the flat and placing it in the ground. The roots are, of course, the most vulnerable part of the plant; many of its fragile root hairs will inevitably be destroyed during the transplanting process, which means that the seedling's ability to gather water and nutrients will be adversely affected until it can grow replacements.

Dig a hole for each seedling, placing it a little lower than the surrounding soil. This little depression will tend to collect and hold rainwater. Give each plant a couple of quarts of water to help it survive the transplanting shock and become established in its new environment.

CUTWORM PROTECTION

An important step at this point is to protect the tender young seedlings against attacks by cutworms. These are the larvae of moths that winter in the soil and emerge in the spring just about the time you're setting out your tasty tomato, eggplant or pepper plants. The cutworms attack these plants at ground level, cutting them off cleanly. To protect your plants, put collars of paper, cardboard, metal, tarpaper or plastic around the plant stems 1" above and 1" below the soil line. Or use a recommended garden insecticide. For very young plants a paper collar is preferred as it lets the surface of the

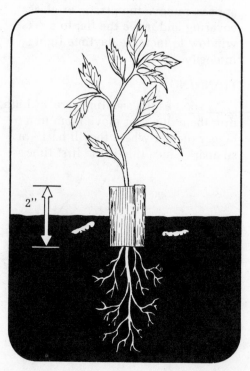

2"

stem dry out and reduces danger from damping-off diseases.

Finally, firm the soil around the plant roots to eliminate any air pockets that may exist. (Air pockets in the soil cause roots to dry out and die.)

PEAT POTS

Considerable transplant shock can be avoided by using individual "pots" or blocks made of peat, moss or other soil material. Many gardeners start their seedlings in these pots, which are set out, pot and all, when the seedling reaches the proper size. Different types are available, including round or square pots, trays, strips, and expanding pellets. CAUTION: When planting these pots, be sure to cover their tops completely with soil. If the tops should be left exposed, a wicking action could occur which could dry out the roots of the plant.

PREPARING THE SEEDBED

In describing the transplant process, we have necessarily gotten a little ahead of our story. The job of preparing the seedbed must, of course, be taken care of before any planting is done, whether of seeds or transplants.

First, it's necessary to determine whether the soil is ready to be worked. Take a handful of soil, squeeze it and drop it to the ground. If it hits the ground with a dull thud and remains in a ball, the soil is too moist and you should postpone your gardening for a while. On the other hand, if it breaks up into little clumps when you handle it or drop it, the time has probably arrived to start work. Heavy clay soils take longer to dry out, of course, than do sandy soils.

Spade up the garden plot to a depth of 8 inches. (As we mentioned previously, you may want to prepare only the ground intended for cool-

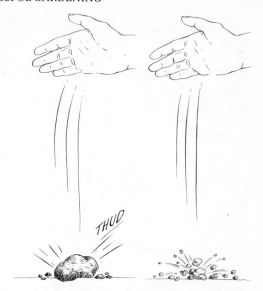

If a clump of earth remains intact when dropped, the soil is too wet for gardening; wait until it shatters (right).

season vegetables at this time, leaving the warm-season area for later.)

Break up the big chunks with a spading fork or rake. Remove any twigs, stones or debris.

If you are fortunate enough to have good, loamy soil you probably won't need to add any soil conditioners, especially if the land has not been used for gardening before.

Soils that are mainly sand or clay can be improved by working in organic matter — 3 or 4 bushels of barnyard manure or compost, or 5 to 6 bushels of peat per 100 square feet of garden. If you planted a cover crop in the fall and have now turned it under, that should take care of soil enrichment at this time.

If organic soil conditioners are added, it's a good idea to wait a week or so before planting seeds. This gives the organic matter time to start decomposing.

PLANTING SEEDS

When the great day arrives for the planting of your garden, there are

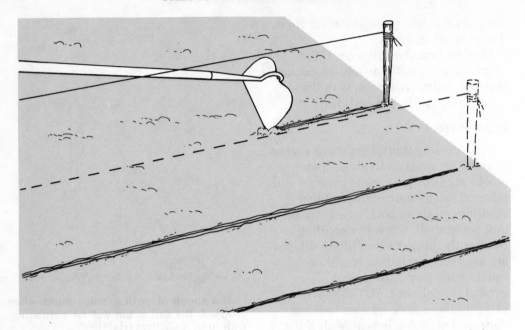

several things you can do to simplify the job:

(1) Rake the surface of the soil well. This top layer of fine soil is important in getting the seeds off to a good start.

(2) Mark off rows by driving small stakes and running string between them. Straight, evenly spaced rows placed at recommended distances make cultivation easier. Many gardeners leave one of the stakes in and fasten a seed packet or other marker on it to identify the vegetable planted.

(3) Using the string as a guide, make a shallow trench or furrow for your seeds. A corner of a hoe or the end of the handle will do the job nicely.

Now you're ready to sow your seed. Most inexperienced gardeners tend to sow too much seed and bury it too deeply. Keep in mind that Nature is constantly reseeding areas all over the world without any digging at all; most seed is intended to lie fairly close to the surface so that it can receive the warmth, light, air and moisture it needs to grow.

Either of two undesirable consequences may ensue if you plant

seeds too deeply: First, any seed that finds itself deep in cold, damp ground may think it's still winter and refuse to germinate. Second, if sprouting does occur, the tiny amount of nourishment built into each seed may not be sufficient to sustain it through a long fight up to the surface, which it must reach before it can create its own food-synthesizing apparatus.

The depth at which most seeds should be planted is easy to remember if you use this simple rule of thumb: Plant at a depth of about twice the smallest diameter of the seed.

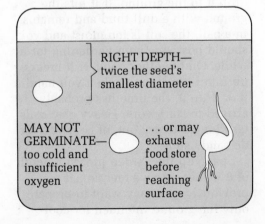

RIGHT DEPTH—
twice the seed's smallest diameter

MAY NOT GERMINATE— too cold and insufficient oxygen

. . . or may exhaust food store before reaching surface

(If you're making late-season plantings in hot weather, you may wish to go a bit deeper where the soil is cooler and more moist.) A common tendency with new gardeners is to sow seed too thickly, especially with the tinier seeds. All this does is waste seed and make the thinning-out job much more time-consuming. It isn't always necessary to use every seed in the packet; in fact, planting seeds so as "not to waste them" actually has just the opposite result: these unneeded extra plants just rob the others of moisture and nutrients, and eventually you thin them out anyway.

Be sure to firm the soil over the seeds, either by treading it down or by gently pressing it with the back of your rake or hoe. Then water the garden well if the soil is dry. But again — don't overdo it; soil that is wet and cold often dries into a hard crust that makes it even more difficult for the young plant to struggle up to the surface.

Incidentally, throughout the growing season it's a good idea to check your garden in the days following rain-storms to make sure no crusting of the soil has occurred. If any sizable crust has formed, break it up to allow penetration of air and nutrients. Various mulches can be used to prevent this crusting of the soil, even newspaper. Solid mulches such as paper or plastic would have to be removed from the rows at the time of germination, of course, (More about mulches later.) Rainstorms also cause new weeds to emerge; get rid of them at once before they grow large and difficult to remove.

COLDFRAMES AND HOTBEDS

One of the simplest and most useful helps a gardener can have is a coldframe — in effect a large box built into the soil with a glass lid on top. One of its purposes is to "harden off" young plants without the bother of bringing them inside the house each night. Another is to permit early starting of cool-season crops: broccoli, cabbage, parsnips, cauliflower. A coldframe will also let you grow lettuce, kale, chard and other crops well into the cold fall months.

Placed in a convenient south-facing location, the coldframe will act as a miniature greenhouse, but its operation

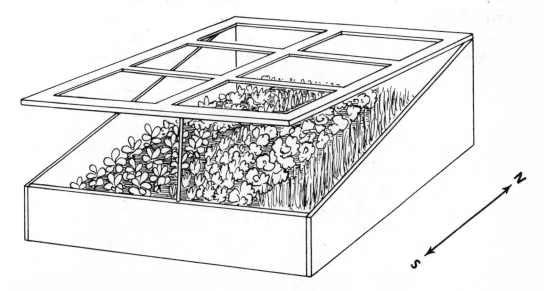

is far from automatic. On a sunny day the temperature inside a closed coldframe could rise high enough to overheat and kill your baby plants, so you have to be careful to prop the glass open and allow ventilation. At night, of course, the coldframe is closed to protect the plants against frost damage.

A coldframe is easy to build. Discarded storm windows and rough lumber will suffice for construction. And if you want to install heat in some manner — electric cable, hot water or steam pipes, or a manure pit — your coldframe becomes a hotbed and can be used for propagation of warm-season vegetables.

SHEET PLASTIC

Another protection device for seedlings is simply a sheet of clear plastic draped over the garden rows and supported by wire wickets. This idea will often enable seedlings to survive unexpected cold spells in the spring, and can also be used in the fall to extend the growing season of leafy crops. Keep a close watch on the temperature build-up under the plastic, however.

THINNING

When the first seedlings appear, it's time to begin the thinning process.

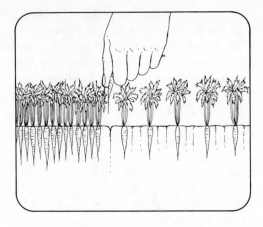

This is necessary in order to reduce the plant population in your garden to the ideal number for vigorous plant growth. Thinning should be a gradual process completed over a period of weeks. The plants should be thinned whenever they have grown to the point where their leaves overlap. Thinning is especially necessary on root crops — radishes, carrots, onions, turnips, rutabagas. If not thinned, these tend to go all to tops. The later thinnings of beets, lettuce and other leafy crops make tasty additions to your salad bowl.

CULTIVATING

Plan to visit your garden as often as possible when the seedlings begin to appear. This is the most critical time of

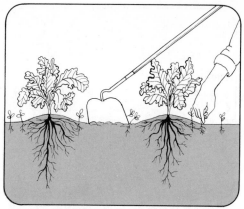

drawing up moisture and venting it into the atmosphere.

Thus regular cultivation (especially after rains) helps assure that your young plants get the full benefit of the water, nutrients, air and sunshine that your garden makes available to them. *If you can, plan to do your garden work in short, frequent visits. This is more fun and it lets you take quick action to correct crusting of soil after rains, bug invasions, disease infestations, and damage by digging or animals.*

their existence, and you can do a lot to help them along. Pulling or hoeing weeds is, of course, the most important operation. Every weed in the garden is competing with your desirable plants for moisture and nutrients. In addition, unchecked weeds will grow to a size where they begin to block off sunlight and impede air circulation needed by your plants. At that stage, of course, weeds are also much more difficult to kill.

If you use cultivating implements, be careful not to penetrate too deeply or work too close to plants; the root systems of many vegetables are near the surface and it's easy to damage them. Weeds in the rows themselves must be pulled up by hand, of course. Cultivating is much easier when it's done promptly. Small weeds are easy to destroy; just a flick of the hoe and they're gone. Large ones are much more work.

CAUTION: In working around tiny seedlings, be very careful not to cover any of the plants with soil; this can kill them very quickly.

Cultivation of the soil not only destroys weeds; it is important for aerating the soil and establishing a dust mulch. The latter is a loose layer of surface soil that acts to slow down the evaporation of water. It does this by breaking up the natural capillary action in soil which is constantly at work

MULCHING

The dust mulch you create when you cultivate the soil is just one of many types of mulch that gardeners use. Nature herself is constantly creating mulch in the form of dead leaves, twigs and other plant material that falls to the ground and acts as a soil covering while it gradually decomposes into beneficial humus.

When your plants have reached several inches in height, they are well enough advanced so that you can safely apply a covering of mulch without danger of smothering them. A three-inch layer of organic material spread between the rows will do a number of things for you:

KILL MOST WEEDS by cutting off sunlight from reaching them.

HOLD DOWN EVAPORATION by blocking off the drying effect of sun and wind.

IMPROVE SOIL BALANCE and add nutrients as the mulch gradually decomposes.

STABILIZE SOIL TEMPERATURES by insulating the soil somewhat from the heat of the midsummer sun. This insulating quality is another reason mulches should not be applied too early in the season; they can keep the soil too cool for proper germination of many crops.

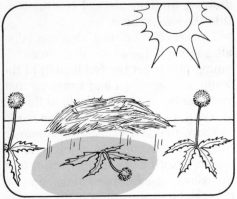

A mulch layer smothers weeds . . .

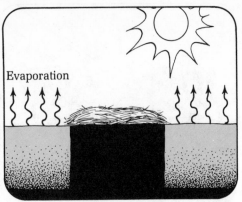

holds down evaporation . . .

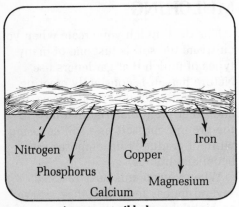

improves soil balance . . .

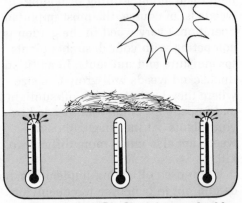

and insulates against both heat and cold.

You will find that the mulch also serves to prevent muddy splashing of your plants during rainstorms, and it helps keep vegetables clean as they develop, especially tomatoes, eggplant, squash and pumpkin.

MATERIALS TO USE

Just about any clean, decomposable matter has been used as mulch at one time or another. The most popular materials are, of course, those that are easily available — leaves, lawn clippings, etc.

Avoid using too much of any materials that tend to compact down and prevent air circulation. Crush, shred and intermix materials so that you have as uniform and loose a texture as possible.

Well-rotted manure makes a good mulch, but avoid fresh manure; it should be aged and mixed with a good quantity of straw before being spread or it may burn plants.

Hay makes a fine mulch, especially salt hay. This is hay cut on salt marshes near the oceans. Gardeners prefer it for mulching because it takes somewhat longer to decompose, has a stiff quality that resists matting, and can be depended upon to be free of weed seeds. Spoiled hay is also popular for mulch use, since it usually costs less because of being unusable as animal feed.

If there are industries near you that process organic matter, you may be able to locate a cheap source of waste materials or byproducts that make fine mulch or valuable additions to your compost heap: spent hops, cocoa shells, fish scraps, sugarbeet residue, corncobs, sawdust, etc.

As the mulch decomposes, it should be renewed. In the fall, turn everything under to improve the soil.

Whenever you turn any kind of organic mulch under the soil, you should add some nitrogen fertilizer. The reason for this goes back to the decomposition process we spoke of earlier. In decomposing, the organic matter uses up quite a bit of nitrogen. Unless some extra nitrogen is supplied, the decomposing organic matter will draw this mineral from the surrounding soil; this may lead to a nitrogen deficiency.

PLASTIC MULCHES

In recent years the use of black sheet plastic for mulching has increased enormously. Some gardeners cover their entire plot with this plastic sheeting after preparing the soil, then punch holes for water penetration and seeding or placing of transplants. (This system is especially useful on stiff clay soils that are hard to cultivate.) Others lay plastic strips between the rows.

Black plastic sheeting is available at most hardware stores in a variety of widths and lengths. Do not use clear plastic; this results in excessive weed growth.

INSECTS AND PLANT DISEASES

Just about every gardener finds evidence of bug invasion or disease at some time or other. With the right controls, applied early enough, you can usually prevent any serious damage to your crops.

You'll find that sturdy, vigorous plants are less likely to develop insect and disease problems, so it's wise to choose disease-resistant varieties if available and encourage healthy growth with regular watering and fertilizing. Thinning is also important — crowded plants have less air circulation around them, and dense foliage tends to increase shade and moisture problems. Good sanitation practices also help — get rid of any accumulations of debris that might harbor disease organisms or attract insects. Destroy any plant that shows signs of disease before it can spread to others.

INSPECT FOR BUGS REGULARLY

It's easy to spot insect damage if you make "bug inspections" regularly. A number of insects are beneficial to your garden, digging drainage canals and air passages that improve the soil's "tilth." But sooner or later you will find signs of activity by harmful ones — chewed leaves, drilled stems, damaged roots. Sometimes the culprits themselves can be surprised at work: caterpillars, beetles, aphids and others are easy to see. Cutworms, borers and slugs are harder to detect because they do their work underground, or inside the plant, or only at night. Some pests are so tiny (nematodes, for instance) that they can be seen only with powerful lenses.

If there are just a few harmful insects on your plants, you may be able to

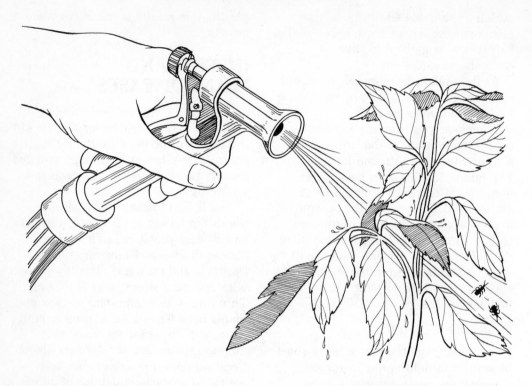

solve the problem by simply picking them off and disposing of them. Or use a jet of plain water to dislodge and wash them off.

If there is considerable insect activity, you may want to spray or dust with the proper insecticides. Because of the great number of these and the variety of application methods, it is best to seek competent advice from your garden store operator or county agricultural extension agent. The important thing is to take corrective action immediately so that you can keep damage to a minimum and prevent further spread of the pests.

Here are some of the most common types of insects:

APHIDS, or plant lice, are tiny soft-bodied insects that suck the sap out of plants, causing stunted growth and curled leaves. Aphids are usually whitish or greenish in color, but also come in brown, red, black, purple and yellow.

Aphids are probably the most numerous of garden pests; this is due in part to their strange reproductive process, which allows unfertilized females to produce generation after generation of other females all summer long; each of these females can also multiply without fertilization. Only in the fall are aphid eggs fertilized; these carry over the winter to provide a starting generation for the next summer's wave after wave of unfertilized females.

Another problem with aphids is the sweet, sticky substance (called "honeydew") that the insects secrete.

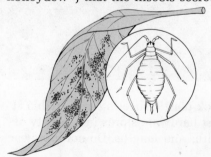

This attracts ants and also forms a culture medium for undesirable fungus growths.

Ladybugs, being natural enemies of aphids, are sometimes purchased in quantities by organic gardeners and released to keep the aphid population down. Unfortunately the ladybugs often have a tendency to move on in search of aphid colonies elsewhere.

MAGGOTS are hard to spot because they attack the roots and subsurface stems of onions, radishes, cabbages, cauliflower, broccoli, brussels sprouts, kale, rutabagas and turnips. Maggots

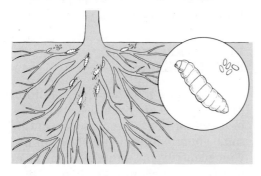

hatch out of eggs laid in the garden soil by flies. The hungry maggots head for the nearest plant root or stem and start feeding. This can result in wilting, yellowing and eventual death of the plants or unsightly tunneling through root crops.

BEETLES come in thousands of forms and they are a threat to plants at all stages of their development. The adult beetles usually feed on foliage and fruit, then lay their eggs either on the underside of leaves or in the stem

of the plant. The grubs or worms which develop from the eggs then feed on the leaves or roots until they are ready to emerge as adults and start the process all over again.

Various beetles and their larvae are especially fond of cucumbers and potatoes. They can also be a problem with asparagus, eggplant, peppers, tomatoes, corn, melons, squash, beans, beets, peas and celery.

FLEA HOPPERS are greenish-black insects about the size and shape of an

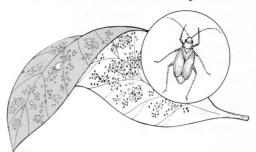

aphid. They suck the sap out of plants like aphids, but hop about like fleas and frequently spread diseases.

BORERS start life as egg masses laid by moths on the underside of a corn leaf (corn borer) or squash leafstalk (squash borer). The eggs hatch into tiny

larvae that feed on the surface tissues of the plant and then burrow into the stalks or ears. There they go into the pupa stage from which adult moths eventually emerge to lay their eggs and keep the cycle going.

CATERPILLARS also develop from eggs laid by moths or butterflies. There are a number of species:

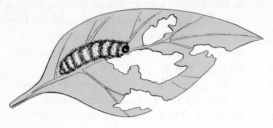

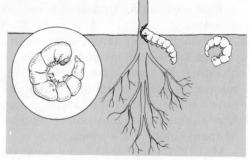

The *cabbage caterpillar* is the most destructive member of the group, and does considerable damage to cauliflower, broccoli, corn, kohlrabi, and brussels sprouts in addition to cabbage. It chews large holes in the leaves which you'll notice immediately. Usually it's only necessary to pick off and destroy these pests.

The *corn earworm* develops from eggs laid in the silks of the maturing plant and gradually eats its way downward to the tip of the ear. (The identical caterpillar, if its eggs happen to be laid on the leaves of a tomato plant, is known as the *tomato fruitworm*.). Another caterpillar attacking tomatoes is the big (up to 4 inches) *tomato hornworm*, which also likes peppers and eggplant.

Leaf rollers are caterpillars you'll find nestled inside of leaves they have formed into cylinders, which become both home and pantry for them.

Webworms also create their own enclosures — a webbing that encircles foliage to form a sort of nest in which the caterpillar lives while it eats the foliage.

Cutworms are seldom spotted at work because they do their damage at night and burrow into the soil in the daytime. Some types of cutworms chew through the stalks of young plants at the soil level; others climb up on the plant to devour leaves and buds. Young plants (pepper, eggplant, cabbage and particularly tomato) are very susceptible to cutworm attack; a hungry cutworm can wipe out several plants in a single night. Young seedlings should be protected with cutworm-foiling collars (see page 36) until the plants are well established.

HOW TO RECOGNIZE PLANT DISEASES

Under most good growing conditions plant diseases are not a serious problem for the home gardener, but if some abnormality should show up in your plants (spots, mildew, stunting or mottling) you should take immediate action to prevent the disease from spreading.

Since there are over 30,000 identified plant diseases we won't attempt a catalog of possible ailments, but rather point out a few signs to look for.

Bacteria, fungi and viruses are responsible for most plant diseases. Other causes are mineral deficiencies, atmospheric impurities, moisture excesses, temperature extremes, or a number of other factors. Linking cause and effect is a job for plant experts; your best bet is to keep a watchful eye on the garden and try to keep damage to a minimum should you find a disease getting a foothold. However, there are two fairly common diseases you should be specifically aware of:

Damping-off is particularly bothersome with young seedlings raised in flats for transplanting. Crowding, overwatering and excessive

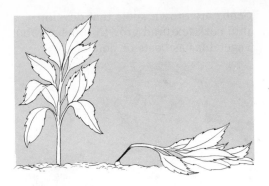

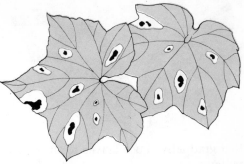

humidity create ideal conditions for the development of a harmful fungus that weakens the plants so they topple over and die. Damping-off can be prevented by using sterilized potting soil and seeing that plants get controlled amounts of moisture, good ventilation and proper thinning.

Blossom end rot is a condition you will find quite often in tomatoes, and it also afflicts peppers, squash and watermelon. It shows up as a leathery scar on the part the fruit opposite to the stem end. It usually appears when the plant is deprived of moisture for any reason shortly after a period of rapid growth. To avoid it, maintain adequate soil moisture and mulch the plants well.

multi-hued, edged with colorful borders, raised, depressed, corky-textured, waxy or slimy.

Mildews form powdery coatings on plants and are most prevalent during wet seasons or where air circulation is impaired.

Other diseases occur far less often, but you should be on the lookout for these evidences of disease infestation:

Spots on leaves and stalks may indicate anthracnose or other spot diseases. The spots can be simply well-defined dead areas, or they may be

Rusts cause reddish-brown spores and pustules to develop on stems and leaves.

Molds are fungus growths that appear as whitish spots or velvety areas

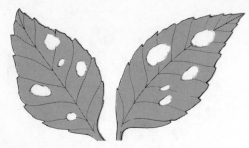

that gradually cause leaves to turn yellow.

Wilts are infections that cause plants to droop, turn yellow, develop streaks and eventually become stunted or die.

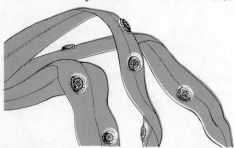

Smuts produce masses of black spores that look like boils or pustules.

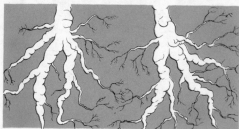

Swellings and contortions of plant roots indicate club root disease, which can cause the plant to wilt and become stunted. The roots may also rot and become foul-smelling.

Scabs are brown spots that develop into cork-textured growths on such root vegetables as beets or potatoes.

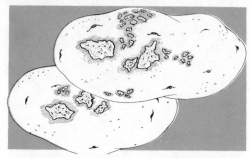

If only a few plants are affected, the remedy is simply to remove and destroy them. In most cases this will arrest the spread of the disease. If the disease is widespread and can't be readily identified, send a sample diseased plant (root and all) to your county agricultural extension agent. Be sure to include as many details as possible about your watering, fertilizing, and any chemical treatment you may have applied. Meanwhile be sure to remove and destroy the diseased plants so that crop damage can be kept to a minimum. (Do not put diseased plant material on your compost heap.)

TOOLS

If possible, resist the impulse to run out and buy a lot of gardening equipment before you know what you really want. Gardening tools are very personal things. Your choice should be guided by your age and strength, the size of your garden, and whether you want to get the job done in a hurry or prefer to putter a bit. Choose the lightest and smallest tools that suit you and your garden. Heavy, cumbersome tools may last longer, but their sheer weight sometimes tires out muscles unaccustomed to garden work. Smaller tools also make it easier to cultivate around plants with less risk of damage.

Be sure to try out different kinds of digging tools particularly. Many people like a square spade for the neat, straight job it does. Others like a round-point spade which can penetrate hard ground more easily and has a longer handle that means less stooping. A spading fork makes it easy to loosen the soil.

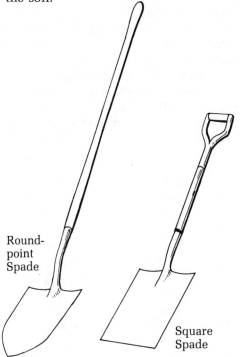

Round-point Spade

Square Spade

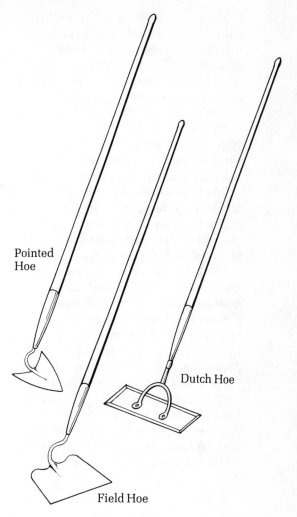

Pointed Hoe

Dutch Hoe

Field Hoe

There are also many varieties of hoes designed to speed the job of cutting or pulling out weeds. Very popular with home gardeners is the lightweight pointed type of hoe with a small heart-shaped blade, useful for opening seed furrows and cultivating in tight areas. Also widely used is the familiar field hoe with its thin, flat blade set nearly at right angles to its handle. Properly used, it does a fine job of chopping off weeds and loosening soil. The Dutch or scuffle hoe has its blade set parallel to the ground, and you alternately push and pull it just under the soil surface as you walk backwards. The square-top hoe has a wider, shallower blade. Particularly useful when working around seedlings is the small hand weeder, with its L-shaped blade only ½" to ¾" wide attached to a trowel-size handle. This tool lets you get very close to tiny seedlings without damaging them.

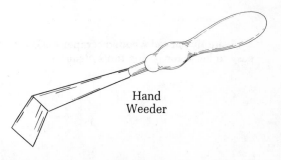

Hand Weeder

Many gardeners consider a wheel cultivator (or wheel hoe) a good investment. This has a number of attachments for soil preparation and weed control. And, of course, a trowel and rake are essential tools for transplanting and seedbed preparation.

The heavy work involved in getting your seedbed ready can be greatly eased by renting a roto-tiller. This machine digs up and pulverizes the soil to the desired depth in a single operation. It takes more physical power to control than does a power mower, say, but it eliminates much of the labor involved in soil preparation.

The principal thing to remember about your gardening tools is that you must keep them clean and sharp for best results. Just a minute or two spent honing the blade on your hoe or shovel will mean a faster, more enjoyable job. An ordinary file is all you need.

Occasionally you'll find that it's simpler to make your own tool to fit a particular need than to try to find one in a store. For instance, it's important after each use of a tool that you scrape off bits of soil and put the tool in a protected place to prevent rusting. You can speed this job by making yourself a small wooden scraper shaped like a spatula. Hang it in a convenient spot where it will serve as a reminder to clean your tools off each time you bring them in from the garden.

Another handy homemade tool is just two broomsticks or dowels on which you wind a length of twine. This device makes it easy to mark straight furrows and plot boundaries. Just unroll the length of twine you need and drive in the sticks while you do your marking. Another trick gardeners use to simplify measuring is to mark one-foot spacings on the handle of hoe or rake.

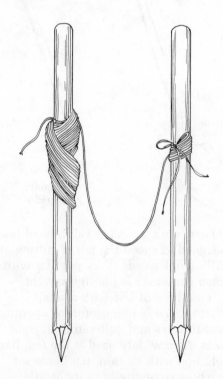

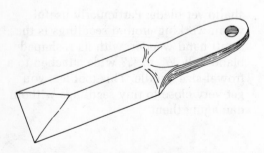

A simply-carved wooden scraper makes it easy to keep gardening tools clean.

Twin stakes and a length of string create a handy row-marking tool.

MAKING THE MOST OF YOUR GARDEN

NUTRITION IN VEGETABLES

"Eat your vegetables" has been the dinner table cry of mothers since time began, and it's the best nutritional advice in the world. The human body needs a regular intake of about 10 mineral elements in order to grow, develop and remain healthy. Vegetables provide many of these in appreciable quantities (see chart) and the garden-fresh taste of home-grown vegetables makes it easier to induce both children and adults to eat plenty of them.

Many vegetables provide roughage needed by your alimentary tract to promote good digestion and prevent constipation. The cellulose or fiber content of vegetables is particularly valuable in maintaining healthy muscle tone in the large intestine.

The vital statistics of many rural and agrarian societies of Europe, Asia and Central America provide interesting sidelights on the effect a vegetable-based diet can have on health and longevity. Most of these so-called "poor" people enjoy better health and a greater life expectancy because of being forced to exist largely on the produce of their own farms and gardens. This is borne out in studies comparing their health records with those of others who have emigrated and become part of western urban societies with diets oriented more toward fats and carbohydrates.

Even the primitive Eskimos learned to supplement their meat diet with minerals and vitamins obtained from the entrails of arctic birds that lived on berries, seeds and vegetable matter.

Nutritionists advise four servings a day of vegetables and fruits, with particular emphasis on those rich in Vitamins C and A. The deep green and deep yellow vegetables are especially high in these vitamins — carrots, broccoli, spinach, kale, leaf lettuce.

Not all the vitamins in vegetables reach the dinner table, of course. Take Vitamin C for example. This is the most unstable and vulnerable of all the vitamins. It is soluble in water, leaches out of foods, is damaged by exposure to high temperatures, light or air. Vitamin C content of vegetables varies with the amount of sunshine received by the crop during the growing season (summer-grown tomatoes have more than twice the Vitamin C of the winter-grown crops). The ability of different vegetables to retain their Vitamin C after harvest also varies considerably — green beans may lose much of theirs within hours; potatoes show a gradual loss over several months. Thus Vitamin C content is far from constant. But here home gardeners have an advantage: they can do quite a few things to cut down on this vitamin loss:

● Rush vegetables from the garden to the dinner table. They will have a far higher vitamin content than the best "fresh" vegetables bought in stores, which could be days away from the parent plant.

● Eat more vegetables raw. That fresh-from-the-garden taste makes it a delight to eat raw cauliflower, turnip, summer squash or other vitamin-rich vegetables in addition to the obvious favorites such as lettuce, tomatoes or peppers.

● Use as little water as possible in cooking, and avoid overcooking.

● Store vegetables in dark areas at prescribed temperatures.

Vitamin A content is also important in vegetables, usually in the form of carotene which is converted to Vitamin A by our digestive systems. Carrots, for instance, have long been recognized for their Vitamin A content. Health food enthusiasts regard carrots highly for

NUTRIENTS IN ONE POUND OF FRESH VEGETABLES
(Based on figures in USDA Handbook No. 8)

	Calories	Protein (grams)	Fat (grams)	Carbo-hydrate (grams)	Vitamin A (Int'l Units)	Ascorbic Acid (milligrams)
Artichoke	16	5.3	.4	19.2	290	22
Asparagus	66	6.4		12.7	2,290	84
Beans, Snap	128	7.6	.8	28.3	2,400	76
Beets	78	2.9	.2	18.0	40	18
Beet Greens	61	5.6	.8	11.7	15,490	76
Broccoli	89	10.0	.8	16.3	6,920	313
Brussels Sprouts	188	20.4	1.7	34.6	2,300	426
Cantaloupe	68	1.6	.2	17.0	7,710	74
Cabbage	86	4.7	.7	19.3	470	169
Carrots	112	2.9	.5	26.0	29,440	21
Chard	104	10.0	1.3	19.2	27,120	132
Corn, sweet	240	8.7	2.5	55.1	1,000	31
Cucumber	65	3.9	.4	14.7	1,080	48
Eggplant	92	4.4	.7	20.6	30	19
Kale	128	14.1	2.7	20.1	29,880	420
Kohlrabi	96	6.6	.3	21.9	70	219
Lettuce, Iceberg	56	3.9	.4	12.5	1,420	28
Lettuce, Looseleaf	52	3.8	.9	10.2	5,520	54
Mustard Greens	98	9.5	1.6	17.8	22,220	308
Okra	140	9.3	1.2	29.6	2,030	122
Onions, Bulbing	157	6.2	.4	35.9	160	42
Onions, Bunching	157	6.5	.9	35.7	8,710	139
Parsley	200	16.3	2.7	38.6	38,560	780
Parsnips	293	6.6	1.9	67.5	120	62
Peas	145	10.9	.7	24.8	1,100	47
Peppers, Bell	82	4.5	.7	17.9	1,540	476
Potatoes	279	7.7	.4	62.8	Trace	73
Radishes	69	4.1	.4	14.7	40	106
Rhubarb	33	1.2	.2	7.6	200	18
Rutabagas	177	4.2	.4	42.4	2,240	166
Spinach	85	10.5	1.0	14.0	26,450	167
Squash, Summer	84	4.8	.4	18.5	1,800	95
Squash, Winter	161	4.5	1.0	39.9	11,920	43
Tomatoes	100	5.0	.9	21.3	4,080	118
Turnips	117	3.9	.8	25.7	Trace	140
Turnip Greens	127	13.6	1.4	22.7	34,470	628
Watermelon	54	1.0	.4	13.4	1,230	15

their beneficial effect on night vision, which is dependent on a good Vitamin A supply. The pigment of the eye's retina (visual purple) is made up of Vitamin A and protein. Exposure to light tends to deplete the pigment's effectiveness unless it is regenerated with new Vitamin A. Without this regeneration, vision in subdued light is impaired. Hence the popularity of carrots (and also spinach, kale, chard and other greens) as a preventive of "night blindness", as it is called.

Vegetables are a prime favorite with people trying to lose weight. There are less than 25 calories in a good serving (2/3 cup) of such tasty vegetables as asparagus, cabbage, cauliflower, celery, cucumber, endive, escarole, green beans, kale, lettuce, mustard greens, parsley, peppers, radishes, spinach, summer squash or tomatoes.

With an intake of less than 50 calories you can enjoy a similar-size helping of beets, broccoli, brussels sprouts or rutabagas. Only a few vegetables have more than 50 calories in a serving, such as corn, beans, onions, parsnips, potatoes and winter squash. And remember, they all contribute minerals, vitamins, and vegetable roughage.

Perhaps the most succinct statement on the nutritional value of fresh produce was made by Dr. Jean Mayer, famed professor of nutrition at Harvard, in his testimony before a Senate committee in 1973:

"If you put foods in order of decreasing usefulness, you would have something like fruits and vegetables, fish, meat, milk, eggs, bread, breakfast cereals, snack foods, candy and soft drinks. Yet, if you look at the amount of money spent in advertising, I think you will note that, generally speaking, the amount is in inverse relationship to the nutritional usefulness of the products advertised."

FREEZING, CANNING AND COOKING VEGETABLES

Freezing is the most popular method of preserving home-grown vegetables nowadays. It's a fast, simple process and when done right it can preserve much of that priceless flavor you enjoy in fresh-picked produce.

Just about any vegetable can be successfully frozen at home except for cabbage, celery, lettuce, watermelon and tomatoes.(Many people do freeze tomatoes, but they thaw to a mushy state suitable only for flavoring soups or stews. Tomato juice freezes well, however.) Be sure to select and freeze only prime specimens — never use over-mature or poor quality vegetables.

To capture maximum flavor, the most important rule in freezing is — don't

delay. If you can't begin the freezing process at once, at least start cooling the vegetables immediately after harvest. Pick them early in the day, when they're at their coolest, and try to get their temperature down under 40°F within four hours or so. At that point, two things slow down remarkably: (1) growth of spoilage organisms, and (2) overripening of the vegetable. Subsequent cooling to the ultimate storage temperature (preferably below 0°F) can be accomplished gradually. Contrary to popular belief, "quick freezing" has little to do with retaining food flavor; the biggest loss of flavor occurs between the time the vegetable is harvested and the moment it reaches that magic 40°F level when organism growth is retarded.

Another point to remember is that just because a package in your freezer is frozen rock-hard, this doesn't necessarily mean it is going to keep well. Water freezes at 32°F, and vegetables are mostly water, so a barely-frozen package can be as hard as a deeply frozen one. Vegetables must be kept at 0°F or lower for best results. At that temperature enzyme action and the growth of micro-organisms are practically halted and vegetables often retain good eating qualities for a year or more.

Select only moistureproof packaging materials when freezing vegetables. Polyethylene is the best type of freezer wrap; avoid the waxed-on-one-side type of paper. Satisfactory containers are wide-mouth jars, new waxed or plastic-coated cartons, or clean used enamel-lined cans with tight covers. Don't use old ice cream or milk cartons, however.

Incidentally, the best and easiest way to seal your polyethylene bags is simply to twist the open end, then apply a rubber band or "twistem".

To preserve vitamin content, most vegetables should be blanched before freezing. Bring water to a boil and place vegetables in it (not so many at a time that you cool down the boiling water. Avoid overboiling or under-boiling; stick closely to the recommended blanching time (see growing instructions for individual vegetables). Then plunge the blanched vegetable into cold water to stop the cooking action, drain carefully, and freeze immediately.

CANNING

If you have the equipment, canning is probably the cheapest and best way to preserve a number of vegetables, especially tomatoes and tomato juice. But avoid "short-cut" canning procedures ... follow traditional methods for safest results. Store cans or jars of preserved food in a cool, dark area to keep contents at their tastiest.

Smart gardeners plan their harvests to allow canning and freezing to be done in short sessions rather than all at once. It's much more fun to process just a few units at a time.

COOKING

The most common mistake in cooking vegetables is *overcooking*. In order to enjoy the matchless flavor of fresh-picked produce it's better to undercook rather than overcook. Even your range setting can influence vegetable flavor — if your cookbook says "Boil for 10 minutes," bring the water to a boil and then *simmer* for 10 minutes. This will tend to keep the vegetables crisper and more colorful. Incidentally, if you like lots of color in your vegetables you can achieve this by simmering them in plenty of water, preferably with no lid on the pot. This will also result in lower vitamin and mineral content, however. The general rule is — use very little water when cooking vegetables. In fact some, such as summer squash, can be cooked using no additional water at all.

STIR-FRYING

This Chinese method of hot-oil cooking brings out the fresh-picked flavor of home-grown vegetables remarkably. Traditionalists insist on using the "wok," a large frypan with sloping sides, but stir-frying is equally successful with an electric frypan or heavy skillet. Vegetables should be cut into thin strips (matchstick thickness) and leafy greens into large chunks. Put three tablespoons of vegetable or olive oil in your cooking vessel, and get it piping hot — almost smoking. Put in the vegetable slices and begin the tossing-and-turning process that cooks the vegetables without destroying their fresh flavor. Not more than four minutes of cooking should be enough to produce tender, delightful morsels.

VEGETABLE STORAGE

Most home gardeners freeze or can their surplus, but you may also want to look into some form of winter storage facility. It isn't hard to devise one, and it can provide you with a supply of fresh vegetables for weeks or even months after the normal growing season ends. Winter storage is only practicable, of course, if:

• Outdoor temperatures in your area average 30°F or lower during the winter.

• You have a storage area with the moisture and temperature conditions required by the vegetables you plan to store.

The main thing to keep in mind in planning winter storage is that vegetables have a natural progression of growth-maturity-eventual decay. Your job is to devise a way of retarding the decay phase of that cycle. With most cool-season root crop vegetables this means keeping them as close to freezing as possible without actually freezing them; this slows up the growth of spoilage organisms to the point where decay is very slow. Others, like winter squash and pumpkin, store best where it's dry and cool but not too cold. Onions, dry peas and dry beans also keep best where it's dry, but they like it a little colder. High humidity is important with beets, carrots, potatoes

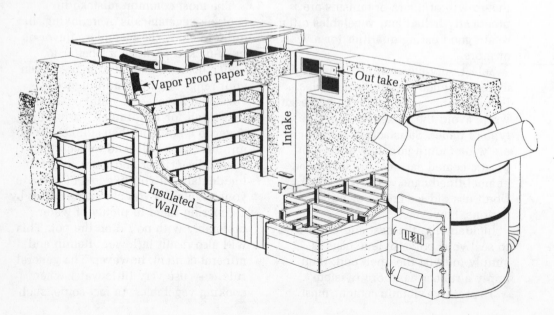

and cabbage; these last longer where it's cold and moist.

Thus you should start by matching the vegetables you want to store with the kind of storage facility you have or can make. This might be an unheated storage room in your home, a pit or storage cellar in the outdoors, or a specially constructed insulated room in your basement. The latter is the best bet for maintaining the uniformly cool, moist conditions (35°-45°F.) required for storing most vegetables. Insulated walls and ceiling plus a ventilating flue to the outside enable you to keep fairly constant temperatures by opening or closing the flue as the outside temperature varies. A floor of slats, sand or brick makes for easy sprinkling of the room when high humidity is desired.

You can obtain detailed instructions for building storage rooms, cellars and pits through state and federal agencies.

Here are the storage requirements of some of the most commonly stored vegetables:

STORE ONLY GOOD QUALITY VEGETABLES

Be particularly careful in harvesting vegetables you intend to store; even slight bruises or scratches can result in fast decay in storage. All except tomatoes should be fully ripe. Check stored vegetables often and remove any that show signs of rotting.

Use these simple tips for best results with specific vegetables:

BEETS AND CARROTS store best in crocks or other containers in cool, moist conditions at around 40°F. Use loose lids or cover with damp burlap to retard evaporation and prevent shriveling; do not seal the containers tightly. Beets and carrots also store well in damp sand, peat or vermiculite. Carrots, beets, turnips, parsnips and rutabagas that you plan to store should not be dug up until just before cold weather sets in. They are better off in the ground until then; light frosts (28°-32°F) will not injure them.

CABBAGE should be individually

Vegetable	Where to store	Recommended conditions: Temperature (F)	Humidity	Storage Period
Beans and peas, dried	Any cool, dry place	25-40°	Dry	Unlimited
Beets	Storage cellar or pit	35-40°	Moist	Fall-winter
Cabbage	Storage cellar or pit	35-40°	Moist	Fall-winter
Carrots	Storage cellar or pit	35-40°	Moist	Fall-winter
Celery	Roots in soil in storage cellar	35-40°	Moist	Fall-winter
Endive	Roots in soil in storage cellar	35-40°	Moist	2-3 months
Onions	Any cool, dry place	35-40°	Dry	Fall-winter
Parsnips	Leave in ground or put in storage cellar	35-40°	Moist	Fall-winter
Peppers	Unheated storage room	45-50°	Moist	2-3 weeks
Potatoes	Storage cellar or pit	35-40°	Moist	Fall-winter
Pumpkin, winter squash	Unheated room or basement	50-55°	Dry	Fall-winter
Rutabagas	Storage cellar or pit	35-40°	Moist	Fall-winter
Sweet Potatoes	Unheated room or basement	55-60°	Dry	Fall-winter
Tomatoes (pink)	Unheated room or basement	40-50°	Dry	1-10 days
Tomatoes (green or white)	Unheated room or basement	50-60°	Dry	1-6 weeks
Turnips	Storage cellar or pit	35-40°	Moist	Fall-winter

wrapped in newspaper to avoid having its undesirable odor absorbed by other vegetables.

ONIONS should be dried outdoors or in a well-ventilated room for several weeks before storage. Discard any that are damaged or have thick necks; these do not store well. Slight freezing will not harm onions if they are not handled while frozen.

PARSNIPS actually improve in flavor if left in the ground. You can even wait until spring to dig them up and eat them. Alternate freezing and thawing can be harmful, however.

POTATOES should be cured before storage. Keep them in a protected shady spot for a week at 60° to 75°F. This will heal skinned areas or small cracks and help prevent decay. If storage temperature goes above 40°F, your potatoes may start to sprout in a few months. Should this happen, simply treat them with a sprout-inhibiting chemical obtainable at garden supply stores.

PUMPKINS AND WINTER SQUASH also require curing before storage. A couple of weeks at 75° to 85°F hardens the rinds and heals surface cuts. Leave a portion of the stem on; this keeps out decay organisms.

RUTABAGAS AND TURNIPS give off odors and should be stored outside if possible. Or store them indoors at 40°F in covered containers of sand or vermiculite. Turnips may also be left in the ground for a considerable period; they withstand quite hard frosts without damage.

SWEET POTATOES should be cured before storage. Keep them at 80° to 85°F for two weeks, then move them to a cooler spot (55°-60°F). Any temperature under 50°F will damage sweet potatoes.

TOMATOES for storage should be harvested just before the first killing frost. Pick all the larger fruit on the vines — ripe, pink, whitish, or green.

Wash and dry them carefully; even casual wiping of dirt can cause sand scarring and subsequent decay. Mature green tomatoes will ripen in two weeks at 65° or 70°F. Reduce the temperature to 55°F and they will take twice that long to ripen. Tomatoes harvested in the pink stage will keep a week or more at 50°-60°F.

COMMUNITY GARDENING

The boom in home gardening has brought a parallel demand for gardening space on the part of apartment dwellers and homeowners whose lots aren't suitable for vegetable-growing. This has led to the development of community gardens in many urban areas.

How do you go about establishing a community garden? There are no set procedures — the principal ingredient of the successful ones seems to be enthusiastic effort on the part of the participants. Often it's just one person who starts promoting a community garden, and once the idea is broached the project takes off on its own.

In one notable instance the wife of a municipal park director balked at the price of peppers in the supermarket and this led to her husband's spearheading the establishment of a community garden on a parcel of unused park land. In another case a corporation set up a "Buzz the Brass" telephone line on which any employee could present a beef or a brainstorm to the company's top officers. One of the first suggestions was a community garden for employees; within months 475 employees were happily gardening during their lunch hours and weekends on a plot adjoining company headquarters.

Just about any sunny plot of land can be adapted for community gardening — odd parcels acquired by highway

departments in the course of road construction, areas adjacent to public buildings, acreages reserved for future expansion by corporations, land unsuitable for development, etc. But care should be exercised to avoid selecting a site having greater than normal problems with drainage, fertility, soil tilth, etc.

Organizing a community garden is mostly a matter of working out plans for plot sizes, rental fees (these range from nothing at all to $5 or so per season), ground preparation, watering facilities and security measures. Here again the participants can provide much of the required manpower — manning plows and tillers, laying out plots, running water lines, organizing plot assignments.

Normally power equipment is used to prepare the ground for planting, and fertilizer may also be applied over the entire garden area (a soil test will indicate what is needed). Once the plots are ready, each gardener assumes complete care of his plot, including watering, fertilizing and cultivating.

Watering is most important to gardening success, but many productive gardens have been developed without pressure water facilities, each gardener carrying water when and if needed. In a dry summer, however, this can get to be quite a chore.

Vandalism (both animal and human) can also be a problem, and some form of security arrangement may become necessary. But many community gardeners report that the large number of people working their gardens, even at odd hours, tends to discourage vandalism.

The public relations value of community gardens has been noted by many corporations, universities and government agencies. Many apartment complexes mention community gardens as well as swimming pools in their sales brochures. In one case a well-known manufacturing company developed a package deal for its employees that included a plot of ground, packets of seeds, a basic gardening guide published by a leading seed grower, and a gardening seminar held by an experienced horticulturist.

The most successful results are enjoyed by community gardens that offer some form of professional guidance for participants. In some cases county agents hold regular "office hours" at the community plots to help with disease, insect, fertilizer, watering and pruning problems. In others local garden-clubbers volunteer to share their gardening know-how.

THERAPEUTIC GARDENING

"If you would be happy for an hour, get drunk; for a day, get married; for life, start a garden"

—*Chinese proverb*

Anyone who has ever grown a crop of any kind knows the beneficial effect gardening can have on a person's mental and physical well-being. The medical profession has long recognized this, and gardening is often prescribed as an adjunct to other treatment. In fact, among doctors themselves there are more gardeners than golfers. The agreeable effects gardening can have on an individual's health were discovered almost accidentally in the early eighteenth century. At that time many hospitals required charity patients to work around the hospital grounds and gardens in payment for their treatment. Then someone noticed that the charity cases got well much faster than the more prosperous patients with identical

ailments. This led to further study which confirmed that gardening could indeed have considerable effect in accelerating recovery. The therapeutic power of gardening has since become broadly recognized and used in many ways. Besides helping patients in all kinds of hospitals and sanitariums, gardening has been prescribed as a relaxing activity for countless people suffering from nervousness and anxiety; caring for a garden has often relieved early symptoms of emotional disorder and may have prevented the development of serious mental troubles in many persons.

Modern urban living is now so artificial and mechanized that the relaxed satisfactions of a garden plot are even more important to a person's well-being than they were generations ago when life was simpler and closer to nature. Today's office or factory worker usually handles only one small function in an enormous complex of activities. This represents efficiency, it's true, but the individual lacks the sense of fulfillment that comes from handling a project from conception to completion. In a garden, he achieves that fulfillment as he watches the seed he has planted gradually develop through the leafing, blossoming and fruiting stages that are part of Nature's master plan.

Gardening is also used as a tool in vocational rehabilitation; success in growing crops can do wonders in restoring a patient's confidence in himself. In prisons, too, gardening can bring about startling changes in the attitudes and general behavior of inmates. And a large school gardening program started a number of years ago in Cleveland, Ohio, is credited with reducing the incidence of juvenile delinquency and crime in that city.

Patients faced with long stays in hospitals or nursing homes find it

easier to adjust to institutional living when they can enjoy an occasional stint outdoors in the garden. Indoor gardening also has its beneficial effects; vegetables and flowers grown in pots and tubs enable even patients with confining disabilities to participate.

Reaction of patients to gardening programs varies considerably, of course. Some aged patients need constant reminders to water, weed, harvest and perform other necessary gardening chores; others seize on the project as a welcome break in the institutional routine and lavish entirely too much care on the plants. The limited attention span of small children is another problem for therapists using gardening as a treatment tool.

One of the most encouraging aspects of horticultural therapy is the change in attitude that often occurs when a patient realizes that the plants he is tending are totally dependent upon him for survival. The sense of responsibility this evokes does wonders for the patient's ego and often leads to a deep interest in gardening that continues after discharge from the hospital.

Horticultural therapy is now a recognized course of instruction at many mental health institutions, and regular programs of gardening therapy are being introduced at hospitals and clinics across the nation. Clemson University, Clemson, S.C. 29631 has been a leader in organizing Hortitherapy Workshops, as their seminars on horticultural therapy are called. The National Council for Therapy and Rehabilitation Through

Horticulture is headquartered at 5606 Dower House Road, Upper Marlboro, Md. 20870.

YOUR COUNTY AGENT

Few city-dwellers are aware that a reliable source of gardening information exists in the person of your County Agent (also referred to as Agricultural Agent, Extension Agent, or Farm Adviser). His function is to disseminate the education programs developed by the State Extension Services, a combined effort of the U. S. Department of Agriculture and the land-grant colleges and universities of the nation.

How these land-grant institutions became established is an interesting footnote to American history. The settlers surging westward in the last century demanded colleges that would meet their practical needs instead of producing only classical scholars. This led to the enactment by Congress in 1862 of legislation permitting the sale of tracts of government-owned land, with the proceeds going to establish at least one college in each state devoted to "such branches of learning as are related to agriculture and the mechanic arts."

Iowa was the first state to implement this legislation, and Iowa State University is one of the oldest and largest of the 70 land-grant colleges in the system.

These colleges at first offered only the simplest courses in practical agriculture and mechanics, but have since expanded into the sciences of mathematics, physics, chemistry, botany, zoology, bacteriology, genetics, nucleonics and engineering.

At the local level, dissemination of the wealth of information generated by the nation's land-grant colleges is the responsibility of the County Agent. He acts as educator, adviser, purveyor of information, executive and local representative of the Agriculture Department. You will find him listed in your phone book. If you have a gardening problem too complex for your garden store operator or County Agent to handle, technical assistance can sometimes be obtained from the land-grant colleges themselves.

Here is a list of them:

ALABAMA: Address your inquiries to the School of Agriculture, Auburn University, Auburn, AL 36380; Alabama Agricultural and Mechanical University, Normal, AL 37562; Tuskegee Institute, Tuskegee, AL 36088. ALASKA: Dept. of Agriculture, Univ. of Alaska, Fairbanks, AK 99701. ARIZONA: College of Agriculture, Univ. of Arizona, Tucson, AZ 85721. ARKANSAS: Division of Agriculture, Univ. of Arkansas, Fayetteville, AR 72701; Pine Bluff, AR 71601. CALIFORNIA: Div. of Agricultural Sciences, Univ. of California, Berkeley, CA 94720; Davis, CA 95616; Riverside, CA 92502. COLORADO: College of Agricultural Sciences, Colorado State University, Fort Collins, CO 80521. CONNECTICUT: College of Agriculture, Univ. of Connecticut, Storrs, CT 06268. DELAWARE: College of Agricultural Sciences, Univ. of Delaware, Newark, DE 19711; Dept. of Agriculture, Delaware State College, Dover, DE 19901. FLORIDA: Institute of Food and Agricultural Sciences, Univ. of Florida, Gainesville, FL 32611; Florida Agricultural and Mechanical University, Tallahassee, FL 32307. GEORGIA: College of Agriculture, Univ. of Georgia, Athens, GA 30601; Fort Valley College, Fort Valley, GA 31030. GUAM: Institute of Resources Development, University of Guam, Agana, GU 96910. HAWAII: College of Tropical Agriculture, Univ. of Hawaii, Honolulu, HI 96822. IDAHO: College of Agriculture, Univ. of Idaho, Moscow, ID 83843. ILLINOIS: College of Agriculture, Univ. of Illinois, Urbana, IL 61801; School of Agriculture, Southern Illinois University, Carbondale, IL 62901. INDIANA: School of Agriculture, Purdue University, Lafayette, IN 47907. IOWA: College of Agriculture, Iowa State University, Ames, IA 50010. KANSAS: College of Agriculture, Kansas State University, Manhattan, KS 66506. KENTUCKY: College of Agriculture, Univ. of Kentucky, Lexington, KY 40506; Kentucky State University, Frankfort, KY 40601. LOUISIANA: Louisiana State Univ. and Agricultural & Mechanical College, Univ. Station, Baton Rouge, LA 70803; Southern Univ. and Agricultural & Mechanical College, Southern Branch P.O., Baton Rouge, LA 70813. MAINE: College of Life Sciences and Agriculture, Univ. of Maine, Orono, ME 04473. MARYLAND: College of Agriculture, Univ. of Maryland, College Park, MD 20742; Dept. of Agriculture, Univ. of Maryland, Eastern Shore, Princess Anne, MD 21853. MASSACHUSETTS:

Agricultural Experiment Station, Univ. of Massachusetts, Amherst, MA 01002. MICHIGAN: College of Agriculture and Natural Resources, Michigan State University, East Lansing, MI 48823. MINNESOTA: Institute of Agriculture, Univ. of Minnesota, St. Paul, MN 55101. MISSISSIPPI: College of Agriculture, Mississippi State University of Applied Arts and Sciences, State College, MS 39762; Alcorn Agricultural and Mechanical College, Lorman, MS 39096. MISSOURI: College of Agriculture, Univ. of Missouri-Columbia, Columbia, MO 65201; Lincoln University, Jefferson City, MO 65101. MONTANA: College of Agriculture, Montana State University, Bozeman, MT 59715. NEBRASKA: College of Agriculture, Univ. of Nebraska, Lincoln, NB 68503. NEVADA: Max C. Fleischmann College of Agriculture, Univ. of Nevada, Reno, NV 89507. NEW HAMPSHIRE: College of Life Sciences and Agriculture, Univ. of New Hampshire, Durham, NH 03824. NEW JERSEY: College of Agriculture and Environmental Science, State Univ. of New Jersey, New Brunswick, NJ 08903. NEW MEXICO: College of Agriculture and Home Economics, New Mexico State University, Las Cruces, NM 88003. NEW YORK: New York State College of Agriculture, Cornell University, Ithaca, NY 14850. NORTH CAROLINA: Schools of Agriculture and Life Sciences and Forest Resources, North Carolina State University, Raleigh, NC 27607; School of Agriculture, North Carolina Agricultural & Technical State University, Greensboro, NC 27411. NORTH DAKOTA: College of Agriculture, North Dakota State University, State Univ. Sta., Fargo, ND 58102. OHIO: College of Agriculture and Home Economics, Ohio State University, Columbus, OH 43210. OKLAHOMA: Oklahoma State Univ. of Agriculture & Applied Science, Stillwater, OK 74074; Langston University, Langston, OK 73050. OREGON: School of Agriculture, Oregon State University, Corvallis, OR 97331. PENNSYLVANIA: College of Agriculture, Pennsylvania State University, University Park, PA 16802. PUERTO RICO: College of Agricultural Sciences, University of Puerto Rico, Mayaguez, PR 00708. RHODE ISLAND: Colleges of Resource Development and Home Economics, Univ. of Rhode Island, Kingston, RI 02881. SOUTH CAROLINA: College of Agricultural Sciences, Clemson University, Clemson, SC 29631; South Carolina State College, Orangeburg, SC 29115. SOUTH DAKOTA: College of Agriculture and Biological Sciences, South Dakota State University, Brookings, SD 57006. TENNESSEE: Institute of Agriculture, Univ. of Tennessee, PO Box 1071, Knoxville, TN 37901; School of Agriculture and Home Economics, Tennessee State University, Nashville, TN 37203. TEXAS: College of Agriculture, Texas A&M University, College Station, TX 77843; School of Agriculture, Prairie View A&M University, Prairie View, TX 77445. UTAH: College of Agriculture, Utah State University, Logan, UT 84321. VERMONT: College of Agriculture, Univ. of Vermont, Burlington, VT 05401. VIRGINIA: College of Agriculture and Life Sciences, Virginia Polytechnic Institute, Blacksburg, VA 24061; School of Agriculture, Virginia State College, Petersburg, VA 23803. WASHINGTON: College of Agriculture, Washington State University, Pullman, WA 99163. WEST VIRGINIA: College of Agriculture and Forestry, West Virginia University, Morgantown, WV 26506. WISCONSIN: College of Agriculture and Life Sciences, Univ. of Wisconsin, Madison, WI 53706. WYOMING: College of Agriculture, Univ. of Wyoming, Univ. Sta. PO Box 3354, Laramie, WY 82070.

37
VEGETABLES
AND
HOW TO
GROW THEM

❧ BEANS ❦

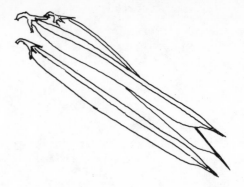

The two most familiar types of beans to home gardeners are the snap bean or string bean (which is eaten in the immature stage, pod and all) and the lima bean, of which only the mature seeds or beans are eaten. Since the latter requires milder climates and longer growing seasons, most new gardeners prefer to raise snap beans (*Phaseolus vulgaris*) which usually produce in quantity over a long picking season. However, the lima types are not difficult to grow and are very delicious.

Another edible-podded type worth trying is the Yard-Long Italian or Asparagus Bean, with very long pods. This is really a bean-like related legume. It requires trellising and a long growing season.

Both snap beans and lima beans have American origins; the concentrated protein content of beans formed an important part of the diet of both Indians and colonists when this continent was first being settled.

Early varieties of the snap bean were fibrous and stringy, but plant scientists gradually developed the tender-podded, stringless varieties popular today.

Snap beans can be grown either as bushes (look for "garden beans" in the seed racks) or as pole-climbing vines (called "runner beans"). The climbing type matures a little later than the bush type, but requires less garden space, is easier to pick, and is usually more prolific. A fence, trellis or strung-cord arrangement about 6-8 feet tall is needed for climbing beans, and they usually require help in getting started up the support.

Never cultivate around your beans when they are wet — that's when bean diseases are usually spread. In watering, try not to moisten the foliage too much. Beans will grow even in poor soil if they get adequate warmth and moisture.

PLANT in well-worked soil, spacing seeds about 1½'' apart in furrows 2 to 3 feet apart. Cover 1'' deep and press soil firmly down. Cultivate soon after seedlings appear (7 to 10 days). They will look like the one shown.

THIN to about 3'' apart when plants are 2'' high.

SPECIAL RECOMMENDATIONS: Beans
are killed by the slightest touch of
frost, so wait until all frost danger is
past before planting them. Soil
temperatures should be around 50°F. or
better. Beans will do best during warm
periods in bright sunshine. About six
feet of row per person will supply
adequate quantities; plant more for
canning or freezing.

FREEZING: Trim ends off washed,
drained beans, cut into pieces and scald
for three minutes. Follow usual
freezing procedure. For canning, omit
scalding.

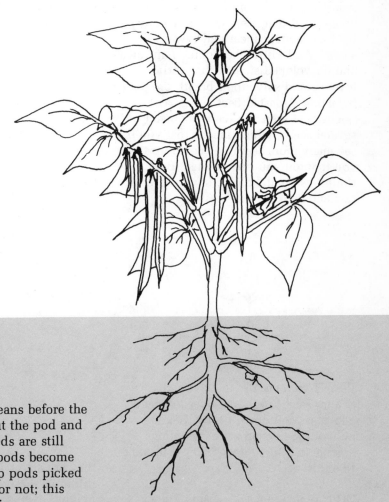

HARVEST your snap beans before the
seeds begin to bulge out the pod and
while both pod and seeds are still
tender. Overly mature pods become
tough and fibrous. Keep pods picked
whether you use them or not; this
keeps the plant producing.

BEETS

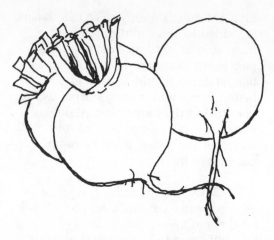

Easy to grow and delicious to eat, beets *(Beta vulgaris, var. crassa)* provide home gardeners with a parade of table delicacies almost from the time they germinate. Thinned-out young plants make nutritious additions to your salad bowl; beet greens are unbelievably rich in Vitamin A. And the young, half-grown beets are famous for their gourmet flavor. Originally found in the Mediterranean area, the beet was at first cultivated only for its leaves. Later it was found that the fleshy root had food value, and was even credited with medicinal powers. Apuleius, a fifth-century quack of sorts, maintained that beets were a remedy for "snakebite, cancer and inward sores." And Pliny, the Roman naturalist and encyclopedist, said that garlic lovers could solve their breath problem by eating a roasted beet.

The beet seed is a really a cluster of several seeds, which means that you'll see many more seedlings come up than you thought you had planted. Beet thinnings are delicious, however, both raw and cooked.

For best flavor, beets should be grown quickly, using ample quantities of garden fertilizer (5-10-5) or well-rotted manure. Slow growth on poor soil results in tough beets.

PLANT in rows 15" to 18" apart. Scatter seed ½" apart, cover ½" deep and press soil down firmly. Begin cultivating as soon as the seedlings emerge in 7 to 10 days. They will look like this.

THIN plants to a 1½" spacing when they are about 1½" high. A second thinning should be made at a 4" height, leaving 3" between plants.

SPECIAL RECOMMENDATIONS: Plant your beets as early as possible after soil becomes workable in the spring; they like cool weather. Midsummer heat may retard germination, but by sowing successive crops at 3-week intervals you will have a continuous supply of young, tender beets throughout the season. Plant at least six feet of row per person, more if you plan to pickle, can or freeze quantities. When picking for table use during early summer, harvest the larger roots for immediate use. This gives the smaller remaining ones more space to grow and develop.

FREEZING: Beets should be blanched and then chilled, peeled and cut before freezing. CANNING: Boil and skin the beets, then trim them and pack into hot jars, adding a teaspoon of salt to each quart. Cover with boiling water and process. Beets are also delicious pickled, of course.

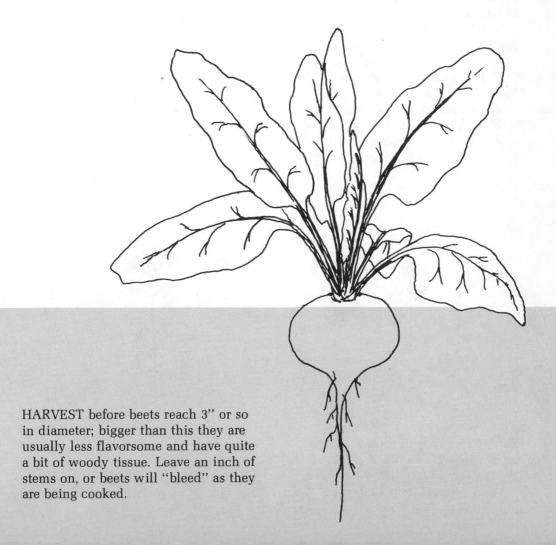

HARVEST before beets reach 3" or so in diameter; bigger than this they are usually less flavorsome and have quite a bit of woody tissue. Leave an inch of stems on, or beets will "bleed" as they are being cooked.

BROCCOLI

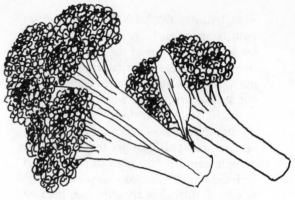

The edible portion of broccoli is its partially-developed cluster of flower buds along with the tender parts of the stem.

The word "broccoli" comes from the Latin *brachium*, meaning arm or branch. A member of the cabbage family, broccoli (*Brassica oleracea,* var. *italica)* develops somewhat branching clusters of buds on thick green stalks. It has been grown in Europe for thousands of years and in this country for centuries, but has only become widely popular here in the last fifty years or so. Before that time it was known and enjoyed mainly by epicures of European origin who grew small quantities in their home gardens, particularly in eastern seaport cities.

Broccoli is a prime source of Vitamin C, and also has goodly quantities of Vitamin A, iron and calcium. Easy to cook, too. Just simmer in very little water and serve with your choice of sauces. Avoid overcooking, since this will cause the heads to separate and flavor will be diminished.

Broccoli takes considerable time to mature—almost three months—but its distinctive flavor when fresh-picked makes the wait well worthwhile for the home gardener.

PLANT sparingly in rows 3' apart. Cover seeds ¼" deep and press soil firmly over row. Cultivate soon after seedlings appear (6 to 10 days).

THIN gradually until plants are 2 feet apart (or space transplants 2 feet apart).

SPECIAL RECOMMENDATIONS: Sow
in open ground as soon as danger of
heavy freeze is past. Broccoli does best
in cool weather. Plant about six plants
per person, more for freezing or
canning.

FREEZING: Select only heads without
blossoms. Wash and trim, then soak for
30 minutes in a salt solution to drive
out any insects. Blanch for four
minutes, chill, and freeze. Broccoli can
also be canned, but sometimes goes off
color and develops a somewhat strong
flavor.

HARVEST while bud clusters are hard
and green, before florets begin to
separate. If kept picked, broccoli will
keep producing till hard frost or early
winter. Take several inches of the
edible stem with the heads; this
stimulates production of side shoots
you can pick later on.

BRUSSELS SPROUTS

One of the few common vegetables of northern European origin, brussels sprouts (*Brassica oleracea* var. *gemmifera*) first became known about 400 years ago. It was developed from a Mediterranean cabbage strain by gardeners in Belgium's capital city, hence the name. In reality a tall-stemmed cabbage, brussels sprouts develops quantities of tiny heads along its stem as it grows.

Brussels sprouts fresh from the garden have a delightful taste with overtones of cauliflower, broccoli and cabbage. Only eight minutes of simmering and they're ready for the table. It's easy to overcook them, so watch the cooking time. This is even more important if you use a pressure cooker — just one minute suffices.

Brussels sprouts are a favorite target of aphids; if you see any on the plants, be sure to dust or spray to keep them out of the foliage and developing buds.

SPECIAL RECOMMENDATIONS: Brussels sprouts thrive best with a long, cool growing season. In late summer or fall, when buds are forming along the leaf axils on the stem, pull off or cut back the side leaves. This allows the buds to form better. An 8-foot row should be sufficient for each person; plant more for freezing or canning.

SOW IN FLATS indoors, following transplant instructions on page 34.

SET PLANTS OUT when all frost danger is past, spacing them 1½ feet apart in rows 3 feet apart. Don't forget cutworm safeguards on tender seedlings.

FREEZING: Remove outer leaves from
fresh-from-the-garden sprouts, then
wash and scald for 4 minutes and
freeze. Brussels sprouts freeze very
well. CANNING: Soak peeled sprouts
in salt water for ten minutes, drain and
boil 3 minutes before canning. Quite
often canned brussels sprouts will
develop a strong flavor and become
somewhat discolored.

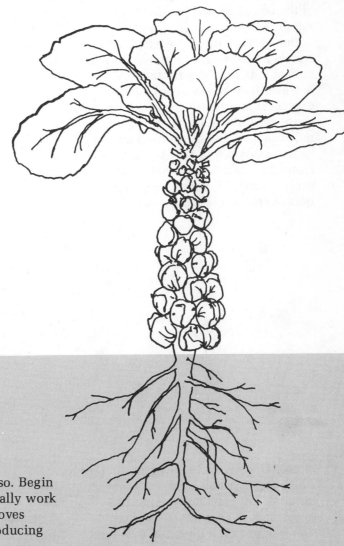

HARVEST buds at 1" size or so. Begin
with lower sprouts and gradually work
up the plant. Light frost improves
flavor; the plant will keep producing
until a heavy freeze.

CARROTS

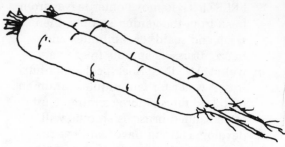

The favorite vegetable of doctors and nutrition experts, carrots *(Daucus carota)* are rich in carotene, or Vitamin A. For many years the carrot was considered only fit for animal feed in this country, but it has a long history of dinner table popularity throughout most of the world. It was first cultivated for its medicinal qualities; later its food value became recognized. European explorers carried the carrot to this continent and it formed a mainstay of the colonists' diet besides being raised by many Indian tribes.

One of our hardiest vegetables, carrots are very easy to grow. They take quite a long time to germinate, however (two weeks or so). Many gardeners mix radish seed with the carrot seed; the quick-sprouting radishes mark the carrot rows and can be harvested before they begin to crowd the carrots. Cultivate your carrots regularly; young seedlings have trouble competing with weeds.

To avoid stunting or malformation of carrots, prepare the soil deeply and be sure all rocks and debris are removed. If you have heavy clay soil, try the stubbier varieties. Water and fertilize regularly if soil is dry or lacking in nutrients; drought and poor soil can result in carrots with a somewhat strong, unpleasant flavor.

PLANT in early spring; carrots can take a light frost. Scatter seeds ½" apart in rows 1½" to 2 feet apart. After two weeks, look for seedlings like that shown, and start cultivating when they appear.

THIN when third leaf appears and plants are 2-3" high. Final spacing should be about 1½-2" apart.

SPECIAL RECOMMENDATIONS:
Thinning is important to achieve
good-sized specimens; do it in two or
three stages rather than all at once. The
seed is very tiny; be sparing when you
sow. You'll have less thinning to do,
and you'll get more produce from each
packet of seed. About 6 to 8 feet of
garden row per person will be adequate
for normal needs. Make a midsummer
planting for a fall crop you can store
for winter. Carrots have very little
insect trouble.

FREEZING: Wash and peel trimmed
carrots, cutting the big ones into
smaller pieces. Scald and freeze.
CANNING: Boil washed, scraped
carrots for 3 minutes before canning.

HARVEST when roots are thumb-size
or larger. After carrots reach 2'' or so in
diameter, their flavor decreases.

❧ CELERY ❧

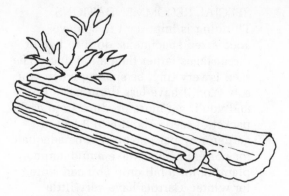

One of the more difficult vegetables to raise, but one of the more rewarding treats from the home garden is celery (*Apium graveolens*). Like many other vegetables, it was first used as a medicine or tonic but people discovered that they enjoyed eating it. By the early 18th century some delicious varieties had been developed and celery took its place as a dinner favorite, both raw and cooked.

Celery requires a long, cool growing season, a deep bed of rich soil, and plenty of moisture. It is usually started indoors; germination is very slow, and seedlings take fairly long to reach the 3" height recommended for transplants.

Avoid watering the celery foliage itself; apply water directly to the ground, and never allow the plants to dry out — this can result in tough stalks.

Celery requires a great deal of patience on the part of the gardener, not only because of its long growing season (5 months from seed) and the finicky nourishing it requires, but also because it only grows well in sustained cool weather; even short periods of temperature extremes can affect its progress.

SOW IN FLATS at a shallow depth — about 1/16". No results will be seen for about three weeks, when seedlings will appear like those shown.

SET PLANTS OUT when they are 3-4" high in rows 3 feet apart, with plants spaced every 10" or so.

SPECIAL RECOMMENDATIONS:
Because of the considerable fertilizing,
watering, climatic and space
requirements of celery, it is not
recommended for the beginning
gardener, or for gardeners with either a
small plot or a short growing season.

FREEZING: Since excellent fresh celery
is generally available all year round,
not many people bother to freeze it. If
you do, just wash and dice trimmed
stalks into 1" pieces, blanch 4 minutes,
chill and freeze.

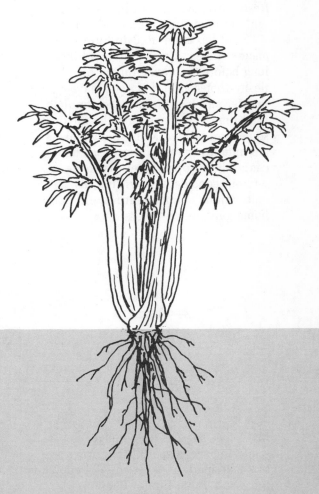

HARVEST young stalks before maturity
if you wish; they're delicious.

❧ CHARD ❧

This is a must for the small home garden and for everyone who enjoys "greens" and fresh salads. Chard is a type of beet (*Beta vulgaris* var. *cicla*) grown for its delicious leaves, which can be cooked like spinach, eaten raw in salads, or added to sandwiches as a lettuce-like filler. The stalk is also very tasty, cooked and eaten like asparagus. Known in some areas as Swiss chard, this prolific plant is achieving widespread popularity not only for its versatility, but also because it provides an almost constant supply of large, fresh leaves which can be harvested without damaging the growing plant.

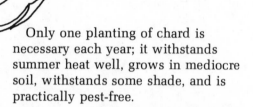

Chard has been used in Europe since ancient times; it was cultivated there long before the development of fleshy-rooted beet types. Its leaves are heavier and less prone to accumulate sand than is spinach, and the flavor is somewhat milder. Many homemakers are unfamiliar with it because chard cannot be shipped great distances without considerable wilting; its cultivation is almost entirely limited to home gardens.

Only one planting of chard is necessary each year; it withstands summer heat well, grows in mediocre soil, withstands some shade, and is practically pest-free.

SPECIAL RECOMMENDATIONS: Young leaves 6-8" across have best flavor. Cut them at the base of the stem and you won't harm the plant. About 6 feet of row is ample for one person; plant more for freezing or canning. For a unique note of color in your garden, try the "rhubarb" variety of chard,

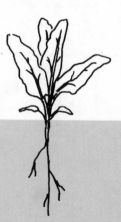

PLANT as soon as frost danger is past, scattering seeds sparingly in rows 1½ to 2 feet apart. Cover seed ¾" deep and press soil down firmly. Begin cultivating when seedlings like those shown appear (7 to 10 days).

THIN to a 4-6" spacing when plants are about 4" tall.

SPECIAL RECOMMENDATIONS: Make several plantings of corn during the season at about two-week intervals. Corn is frost-sensitive, but you may want to risk an early planting in the hope of enjoying the delights of early corn. Normally you would wait until all frost danger is past, however. Plant in solid blocks rather than long rows for better pollination. Twenty-five feet of row will produce enough for one person; plant more for freezing and canning.

FREEZING: For whole-ear freezing, choose varieties with small ears and narrow cobs, such as some of the midget varieties. Husk and de-silk freshly-picked ears, then blanch for 10 minutes. Chill and freeze. For whole-kernel corn, (the preferred method) use large-eared varieties with deep kernels; blanch cobs for 4 minutes before slicing kernels off. CANNING: Husk, de-silk, wash and arrange ears by size for easier canning.

HARVEST when the ears have tips that become blunt and rounded, with developed kernels that spurt a juice when squeezed with a nail.

CUCUMBERS

This popular vegetable (*Cucumis sativus*) originated in the shadow of the mighty Himalaya Mountains of northeastern India and is believed to have been carried to the western civilizations long before written history. Its enthusiasts have been many over the centuries; both Tiberius and Charlemagne were cucumber aficionados, and Columbus rightly guessed that the New World climate would be ideal for cucumber production. In fact, several decades after Columbus introduced cucumbers to the island of Haiti, the explorer DeSoto reported finding the Indians of Florida growing cucumbers "better than those of Spain."

The two main types are the *slicing varieties*, preferred for salad use because of their longer shape, and the *pickling varieties*, which are prolific producers of the smaller fruits usually harvested in the immature stage. Both types can be used for either purpose; if you're growing cucumbers for pickling, harvest while the fruits are still small.

If for table use, let them grow larger, but not to the point where they turn yellowish or whitish and become seedy inside. Look for the new hybrid varieties; they are far more productive and disease resistant. Of particular interest are the new gynoecious varieties, which have all female or pistillate plants. (With cucumbers, the male blossom appears first, but produces no fruit. Only the later-blooming female blossoms produce cucumbers, and these "all-girl" varieties thus yield a bigger harvest.)

PLANT seeds 4" apart, or in hills of 6 to 8 seeds, each hill or row 4 to 6 feet from the next. Cover ½" deep and firm soil well. Cultivate when seedlings appear (in a week or so).

THIN when plants are 2" tall. [gradually until plants are a foc (or 3 to a hill).

SPECIAL RECOMMENDATIONS:
Cultivate carefully to avoid cutting
plant roots near the surface. Trellis to
save space. When harvesting, simply
roll the vines over and pick — never
lift them high or they may tear. Treat
the vines carefully and they will bear
longer. Plant one or two hills per
person, waiting until all danger of frost
is past; cucumbers can't take cold
weather. When pickling, use only the
small-to-medium sizes and pickle
within a day or two of harvest for best
flavor.

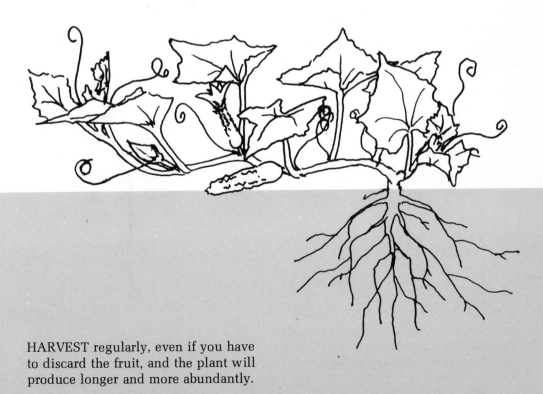

HARVEST regularly, even if you have
to discard the fruit, and the plant will
produce longer and more abundantly.

EGGPLANT

Here is a vegetable with a colorful history. Believed to have originated in the Burma area, it acquired quite a bit of folklore as it spread into the upper European regions. Botanists there somehow became convinced that eating eggplant would cause insanity; they ignored its botanical name (*Solanum melongena*) and dubbed it *Mala insana*, meaning "mad apple." The more romantic Spaniards called it *berengena*, or "apple of love," being convinced the eggplant had aphrodisiac qualities.

The name "eggplant," by the way, stemmed from the fact that early varieties (many of which are still popular in other parts of the world) produced small, egg-shaped fruit.

A relative of the tomato and pepper, the eggplant has similar needs with respect to climate and cultivation. It is strictly a warm-weather vegetable, usually raised by the transplant method. The eggplant's undeniable good looks make it a fine addition to any garden; you'll be proud of its large purplish-black fruit. In addition, its pleasant, mild flavor combines well with companion vegetables and delicate seasonings to create memorable casseroles and other dishes.

SPECIAL RECOMMENDATIONS: Once fruits have set and are beginning to develop, pick off all further blossoms and terminal growths to leave only four or five fruits to mature. Inspect plants regularly for insect invasion; watch for defoliation and check underside of leaves especially.

SOW IN FLATS about 8 weeks before you plan to move the seedlings outside. Germination normally takes 10-15 days, but occasionally requires as long as a month.

SET PLANTS OUT only after frost danger is well past and soil is warmed up. Apply cutworm safeguards.

FREEZING: Peel, slice and soak in salt
water for a half-hour to prevent
darkening of flesh. Scald for 4½
minutes in salt water, chill, drain and
package. CANNING: Wash and pare
freshly-picked eggplant, then cut into
slices or cubes and immerse in cold
water for an hour. Drain, boil for 5
minutes, can.

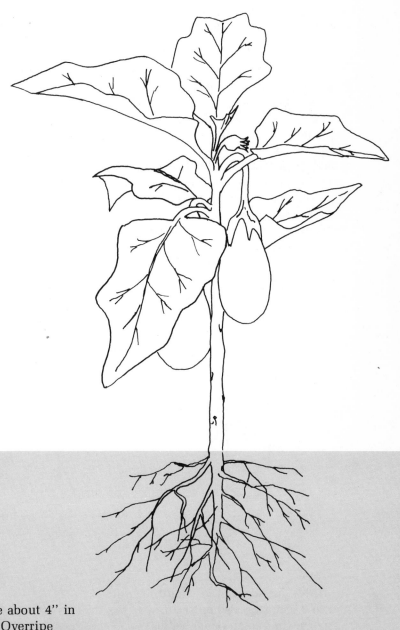

HARVEST when fruits are about 4" in
diameter and still glossy. Overripe
fruits have a dull color and bitter seeds.

❧ KALE ☙

Kale is very similar to collards — in fact it has the same botanical name (*Brassica oleracea* var. *acephala*), which means "cabbage without a head." But in one respect there is a great difference: kale refuses to grow well in hot weather, whereas collards will survive although developing an unpleasant flavor.

Kale is a powerhouse of minerals and vitamins, outperforming even carrots in the important Vitamin A department. Many gardeners like to plant a late crop, since it will supply greens during the fall months when other leafy vegetables have ceased to produce. It is also an attractive and versatile plant; if you're short of gardening space, try putting a few kale plants in among your flower borders. There are several varieties that produce plumelike leaves with interesting fringes; some are so decorative that they find their way into flower arrangements.

Because kale does best in quite cool weather, many gardeners use transplants to take advantage of the first cool weeks of spring. It can be grown practically all winter in areas where the ground doesn't freeze.

PLANT sparingly at ½" depth in rows 2 to 3 feet apart. When seedlings appear (in 6 to 10 days) begin cultivation.

THIN to 12-15" spacing when plants are about 2-3" high. The thinnings are delicious.

SPECIAL RECOMMENDATIONS: Since
kale is a member of the cabbage family,
it is susceptible to similar insect and
disease infestations. Inspect plants
regularly and take corrective action if
necessary. How much to plant: a four-foot
row per person will be adequate.

HARVEST the outer leaves at any time;
the plants will keep growing all season
long, and flavor actually improves after
the first light frosts.

LETTUCE

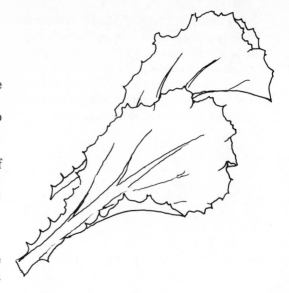

It is in growing lettuce that the home gardener probably has the biggest advantage over his neighbors limited to supermarket produce. Lettuce (*Lactuca sativa*) attains its finest flavor and highest vitamin content in the looseleaf varieties largely bypassed by commercial growers in favor of the less perishable iceberg heading types. The looseleaf varieties were the most primitive cultivated kind, and their superior flavor doubtless helped lettuce achieve its worldwide predominance in salads. Herodotus mentions lettuce being served to Persian kings in the sixth century B.C.; by the beginning of the Christian Era there were a dozen varieties in cultivation by the Romans. One of their favorites was Romaine (or Cos), hence its name. This popular variety forms a distinctive rosette of long, flavorful leaves and is finding increasing favor as a pretty addition to the family salad bowl.

Some enjoy raising the familiar heading type (such as Iceberg), but because of its ready availability in supermarkets and its rather unexciting flavor most home gardeners opt for the looseleaf varieties (Grand Rapids, Black Seeded Simpson, Salad Bowl, etc.) which are easiest to grow, earliest to reach harvestable size, and richest in vitamins.

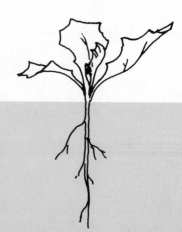

PLANT as soon as soil can be worked, scattering seed sparingly in rows 15" apart. Cover ¼" deep and firm soil well.

THIN OUT seedlings to a 4" spacing (loose-leaf varieties) or 8" spacing (heading varieties). The thinnings are delicious.

Also very popular are the Bibb varieties, small butter-head types that are early to mature and have a very distinctive, delicate flavor.

Lettuce is a fast-maturing crop that is ready by early summer, so get it in the ground early. If you wait too long, summer heat may cause the plants to bolt (go to seed prematurely).

SPECIAL RECOMMENDATIONS: Cultivation around lettuce should be quite shallow to avoid injuring roots; don't go down more than an inch or so. Lettuce will tolerate a location in partial shade if you're cramped for space.

HARVEST head lettuce when center firms up. With loose-leaf varieties, pick outer leaves as plant develops and cut off mature plant a couple of inches above the ground; it will often reward you with new leaves.

MUSKMELON

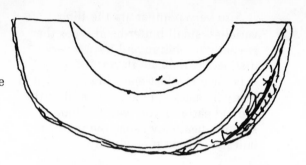

The netted muskmelon or cantaloupe (*Cucumis melo* var. *reticulatis*) is a member of the gourd family that includes the pumpkin, squash, cucumber and watermelon. The muskmelon is a native of the Middle East with a history that goes back thousands of years. It was in cultivation across the entire Eastern Hemisphere when Columbus brought the first muskmelon seeds to the New World in 1494. By the middle of the following century it was being grown by settlers and Indians from New England to Florida.

Plenty of sunshine, plenty of space and plenty of water are required to develop melons with the size and sweetness you want. However, if your growing season is too short to allow leisurely development, you may be successful with one of the new early-maturing hybrids now available.

Melons grow best in well-drained, fertile soil, somewhat to the sandy side. In the far northern regions with very short growing seasons it is necessary to start seedlings indoors. Since melons are easily damaged in transplanting you should use peat pots or containers that are large and deep enough to permit good root development. After moving the seedlings outdoors, be sure they are shielded against cold winds with protective caps, boards or panes of glass until they are well along.

PLANT in warm soil after all frost danger is definitely past. Plant 6 to 8 seeds ½" deep in hills (groups) 6 feet apart, or in rows with seeds spaced every 4 inches. After 6 to 10 days, look for seedlings like those shown.

THIN to the best 2 or 3 plants in each hill; space row-planted seedlings every 2 feet (this also applies to transplants).

SPECIAL RECOMMENDATIONS:
Beetles are quite fond of melons in the
young seedling stage. If they appear, be
sure to dust or spray with the proper
remedy. In the South during damp
weather mildews may develop; this
requires a dusting of the proper
fungicide. Nematodes can also be a
problem in certain soils, and this can
only be controlled with a specific
nematocide or soil fumigant—ordinary
insecticides are usually not effective.

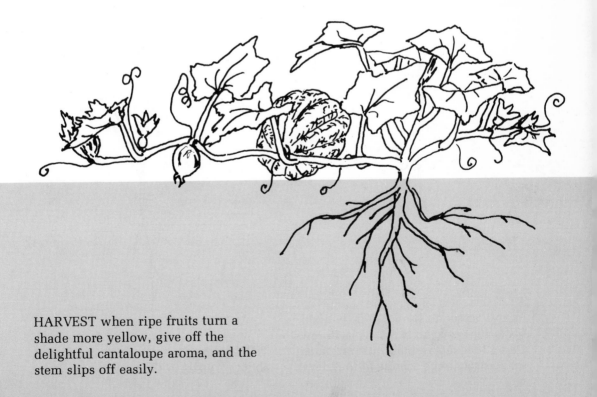

HARVEST when ripe fruits turn a
shade more yellow, give off the
delightful cantaloupe aroma, and the
stem slips off easily.

MUSTARD

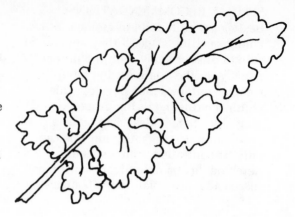

Indian mustard (*Brassica juncea*) is the type most often raised in this country, being easier to grow and more heat-tolerant than the less pungent Chinese Cabbage (*Brassica chinensis*) preferred by some for salad use. Indian mustard is available in a number of both plain-leaved and curly-leaved varieties; it is increasing in popularity as a somewhat stronger-flavored substitute for spinach in many cooked dishes.

Mustard thrives in cool weather and matures fast. Plant it early enough so that you can harvest it before the arrival of midsummer heat; that can cause it to go to flower and seed very quickly.

Mustard adds an interesting flavor to salads, and is also delicious boiled (use very little water). For maximum vitamin content, use the greens fresh from the garden, or refrigerate them as soon as you pick them.

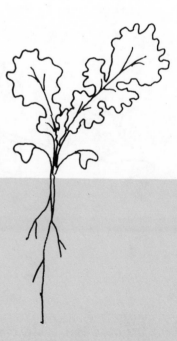

PLANT as soon as soil can be worked, scattering seed thinly ¼" deep in rows 1½ to 2 feet apart. Start cultivation as soon as seedlings emerge (4 to 5 days).

THIN gradually until plants are spaced about 6" apart in the rows.

SPECIAL RECOMMENDATIONS: Plant
another crop in midsummer for fall
use. If you see aphids or cabbage
worms, hose them off or apply dusts or
sprays.

FREEZING: Pull the leafy part from the
stalk, wash, scald for 3 minutes, chill,
and freeze. CANNING: Pick small,
tender leaves and wash thoroughly.
Heat until wilted, cut through several
times and can.

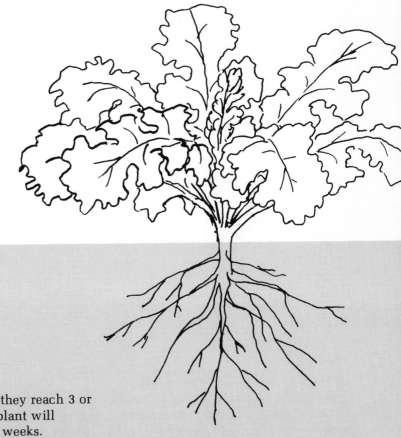

HARVEST leaves when they reach 3 or
4 inches in length; the plant will
continue to produce for weeks.

❧ OKRA ❧

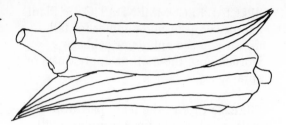

This African import is another off-beat vegetable that can offer home gardeners a novel treat. Largely unappreciated in the north, okra (*Hibiscus esculentus*) is a fast-growing plant whose young pods must be harvested promptly; they can become too old and tough in a matter of days. Picked and eaten at their height of flavor and tenderness, young okra pods are a delight. In soups and stews, of course, okra is a familiar favorite, especially in the South.

Okra grows as a large, bushy plant with lush, exotic-looking leaves. Its requirements are somewhat similar to those of corn: plenty of warmth, sunshine — and space. Okra is particularly sensitive to frigid winds. In colder climates, gardeners often place their okra plants in some sheltered location — on the sunny side of buildings or fences, for instance.

Unseasonably cool summers can bring very poor results. Transplants are recommended in northern regions. Germination can sometimes be hastened by soaking the seeds for a day or so before planting.

PLANT in warm soil, scattering seed thinly in rows 3 feet apart and covering ½" to ¾" deep. Start cultivation when seedlings appear (15 to 20 days).

THIN OUT when plants are 2-3" high until spacing is 1-1½ feet between plants. Do it gradually.

SPECIAL RECOMMENDATIONS: Use
aluminum utensils when cooking okra;
other metals may cause a harmless
discoloration of the pods. Keep pods
picked off or the plants will stop
producing.

FREEZING: Remove stems and
blossoms from young, tender pods,
wash and drain, then scald 3 to 4
minutes, chill, and freeze. CANNING:
Boil washed and drained pods for just
a couple of minutes before canning.

HARVEST when pods are not more
than 3" long. If the stem resists a sharp
knife, the pod is probably past its peak
of flavor.

❧ ONIONS ❧

Here is a vegetable which, along with its flavorsome cousins — garlic, leek, shallot and chive — is welcomed into every household where gourmet cooking is an art. The onion *(Allium cepa)* originated in Asia and has been cultivated since prehistoric times. It crossed the Atlantic with the Spanish explorers and soon became a mainstay in the diets of both Indians and colonists.

There are two main types: *bunching onions,* that you pick and eat in the early green stage, and *bulbing onions,* which you allow to mature before harvesting.

There are three popular ways of raising onions:

SEED: Those raised from seed have superior flavor for fall harvest and keep best in winter storage. The seed-raising method is illustrated below.

SETS: Onion sets are the small partially-developed onion bulbs you plant for early green onions or late summer bulbs. These sometimes do not store as well as seed-raised onions, depending on variety grown.

PLANTS: Used for raising long-season Bermuda and Sweet Spanish onions, very mild and sweet. These mature before seed-grown kinds but are not as long-lasting in winter storage.

PLANT seeds as soon as soil can be worked in spring. Sow at ½" depth in rows 18" apart. Seedlings will appear in 8 to 12 days.

THIN to 3" apart when seedlings are 3" high. Add the thinnings to your salad bowl.

SPECIAL RECOMMENDATIONS: Give
onions plenty of light and air; pull
weeds by hand to avoid heaping dirt
around plants. Knock down tops at the
bulb neck before harvesting if you plan
on winter storage. Six feet of row per
person will be adequate, but onions
store so well that most people plant a
good deal more. Freezing or canning is
usually unnecessary.

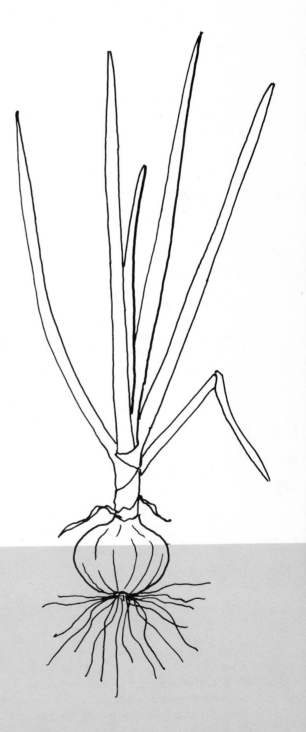

HARVEST only after the tops have
ripened and the outer skin has dried.
Pull bulbs gently and leave them on
the ground to dry for a few days.

PARSNIPS

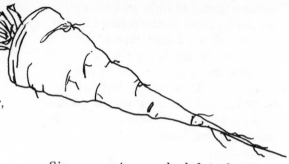

Do parsnips (*Pastinaca sativa*) deserve a spot in your garden? If you've ever tasted a home-grown parsnip harvested at its peak of flavor, your answer will be an enthusiastic "Yes!". Unfortunately, most people have only eaten overage specimens, which can often develop a rather disagreeable taste. Ideally, parsnips should be allowed to develop in the cold ground of fall and early winter, which turns their starch deposits into sugar and results in a sweet, nutlike flavor. So memorable is this taste that the Emperor Tiberius had regular supplies brought in from Germany.

Parsnips form a very long, deep, tapering root and consequently do best in fairly loose soil. If planted in heavy clay soils they may be somewhat difficult to harvest; the crowns are quite brittle and this, combined with the deep roots, makes it necessary to harvest with a spade or fork in order to loosen the soil around the roots.

Since parsnips can be left in frozen ground indefinitely, they are often planted late for a harvest that lasts from fall until the next spring. In mild climates you can plant them in the fall for spring harvest.

PLANT in deeply spaded soil, scattering seed sparingly in rows 1½-2' apart. Cover with ½" of soil and tamp well. When seedlings appear (2-3 weeks) begin cultivation and keep soil moist.

THIN seedlings to a 3" spacing when they are about 3" tall.

SPECIAL RECOMMENDATIONS: Soak
seeds in water for 24 hours before
planting to speed germination. Plant
about five feet of row per person.
Parsnips seldom have insect or disease
problems.

FREEZING: Remove tops from smooth,
firm roots free from any woodiness.
Wash, peel and cut into chunks or
slices. Blanch 3 minutes, chill, drain
and freeze.

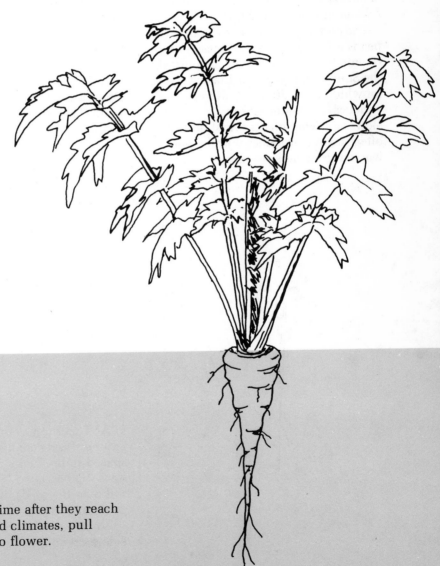

HARVEST at any time after they reach
a good size. In mild climates, pull
before tops begin to flower.

PEAS

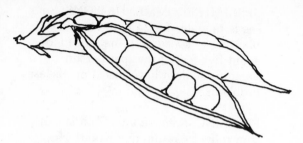

The pea *(Pisum sativum)* has been a favorite in Europe since the Stone Age. It was cultivated in many areas and achieved various forms — tall, short, bushy, compact, smooth-seeded, wrinkle-seeded — and many colors. The English finally developed modern peas (and the technique of eating peas with a knife). In our southern states, these kinds are referred to as "English peas" to distinguish them from the cowpeas or Southern peas *(Vigna Sinensis)* that are popular there but are seldom grown in the North.

The common or "English" garden pea is a fast-growing cool-season crop ripening in early summer. In contrast, the Southern, cowpea or Blackeye types (of which there are many different varieties) are warm-season, slower-growing plants found more often in southern areas with longer, warmer growing seasons.

In deciding the variety you wish to plant, keep in mind that the heavy-yielding, large-podded pole varieties (Alderman or Telephone, for instance) require a fairly long period of cool weather. If you don't have conditions like these, consider planting dwarf varieties (such as Little Marvel or Wando or Perfection) which mature much faster and don't require trellising, but are not as prolific.

Another possible choice is one of the new edible-podded varieties such as Dwarf Gray Sugar or Chinese Edible Pod. These are harvested early and eaten pod and all.

PLANT as soon as the frost is out of the ground. Seeds are big enough to be spaced individually about 2" apart in rows 2-3 feet apart. Firm about 1½" of soil over the seeds, which should germinate in 6 to 10 days.

Provide support for pole varieties before climbing tendrils form.

SPECIAL RECOMMENDATIONS: It's especially important to avoid high-nitrogen fertilizers with peas; they will respond with too much vegetative growth. Plant about 12 feet of row per person, more if you plan to freeze or can some.

FREEZING: Shell and scald tender, mature peas, chill in cold water and freeze promptly. Skins tend to toughen if you delay. With sugar or edible pod varieties, the entire pod is processed, of course. Remove any fibers on the upper margin of the pod. CANNING: Because of the high protein content of peas, canning is only recommended if extreme precautions are taken.

HARVEST when the pods have become almost rounded. Pick often, and don't miss any; overripe pods retard production if left on the vine. Hold the vine while picking to avoid tearing it.

PEPPERS

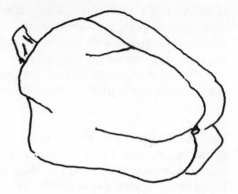

Early explorers of the Western Hemisphere brought a strange new vegetable back to Europe with them — the fiery peppers that the Indians of the Southwest and Mexico consumed in great quantities. Many different types were included — now known as cayenne, chili, etc. — but the one that ultimately became the favorite of home gardeners is the bell pepper *(Capsicum annuum)* with its mild, distinctive flavor. These large-fruited sweet peppers (such as California Wonder) are green till they become fully mature. Then most varieties ripen to red and a few to yellow or orange. Blocky in shape and thick-walled, they are best for stuffed peppers, casseroles or salads.

The pungent hot varieties (such as cayenne) are usually smaller-sized, often narrow, tapering or conical in shape with thin walls. These are used for chilis, hot dishes, etc.

Peppers produce nicely-structured plants with attractive foliage and neat white flowers. For this reason they are often grown in flower beds or borders.

SEED IN FLATS about eight weeks before the last frost is expected. Germination takes 10 to 14 days. Peppers are sensitive to transplant shock, so use of peat pots is advisable.

MOVE SEEDLINGS OUTDOORS when all frost danger is past. Choose a sunny location. Set plants 2 feet apart in rows 3 feet apart.

SPECIAL RECOMMENDATIONS:
Peppers store best if you leave a
half-inch of stem on as you harvest
them. Don't pick tiny peppers; they're
not very good to eat. Wait until they
are good-sized, even if still green. Keep
peppers picked off for greater
production. About six feet of row per
person will be adequate; plant more for
freezing, canning or pickling.

FREEZING: No blanching is necessary;
just slice up freshly-picked bell
peppers after removing stems, seeds
and inner white ribs. Then freeze.
CANNING: Boil similarly prepared
whole peppers for 3 minutes and can.

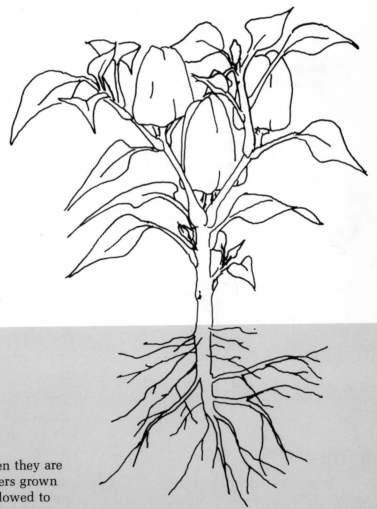

HARVEST bell peppers when they are
firm to the touch. Hot peppers grown
for dry storage should be allowed to
ripen fully on the vine.

POTATOES

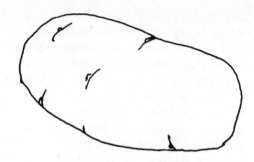

The important thing in growing Irish potatoes *(Solanum tuberosum)* is to plant only certified seed tubers. The potato has a very long history of susceptibility to disease, a failing that has had historic consequences. The famous epidemic of potato late blight that occurred in Ireland in 1846 resulted in near starvation of the population and a mass migration to the New World.

Your climate will determine the eating quality of the potatoes you grow. Storage of starch in the underground tubers, which results in the mealy quality most people like, is apparently influenced by cool nights. Thus the upper tier of states is most likely to produce potatoes with superior eating qualities. Each section of the country has its own favorite potato varieties, however.

You usually won't find potato seed in any store; what you plant is an egg-sized chunk of a potato grown for seed or propagation purposes and certified as disease-free. (Never use leftover supermarket-purchased potatoes you may have on hand.) Each chunk you plant should have one or two "eyes" (miniature buds) on it.

SPECIAL RECOMMENDATIONS: For best storage qualities, leave potatoes in the ground until vines are completely dead. Dig them in cool weather when soil is dry to avoid scalding. Potatoes require a great deal of space and are susceptible to many diseases. Grow only if you have extra garden space or if you want a few new potatoes in midsummer. Decide for yourself if you have the garden area and patience to devote to a crop. Each person will require about 8-10 hills for a good supply.

PLANT in warm, dry soil placing each chunk 5" deep with the eyes up. Firm up a mound of soil around each one.

KEEP MOUNDING SOIL around the tubers as they develop. If exposed to light their skin will turn green, bitter and mildly poisonous.

FREEZING: Wash, peel, and remove
deep eyes, bruises and green surface
coloring. Cut into half-inch cubes and
scald 5 minutes. Chill and freeze
immediately. (French fries and hash
browns can also be frozen
successfully.) Since potatoes normally
store so well under cool, moist conditions,
freezing is not usually necessary.

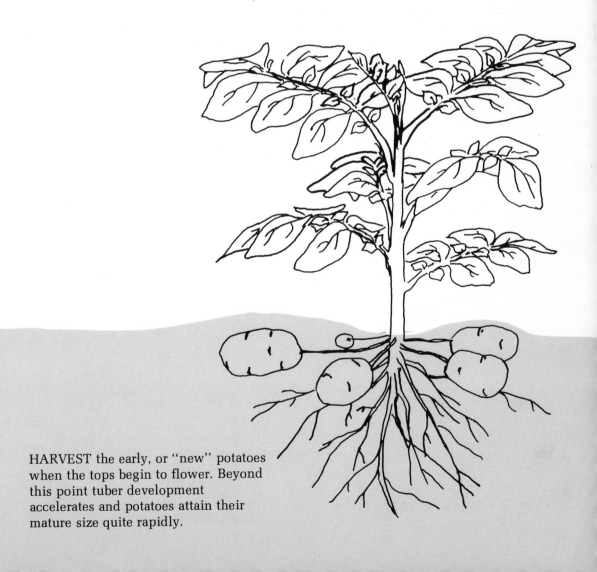

HARVEST the early, or "new" potatoes
when the tops begin to flower. Beyond
this point tuber development
accelerates and potatoes attain their
mature size quite rapidly.

RADISHES

The botanical name for the radish is *Raphanus sativus*, derived from a Greek word meaning "easily reared," and this pretty well describes why the radish finds a place in most gardens. The ancient Greeks went overboard in their admiration for radishes, even making little gold replicas of them, and this pleasantly pungent root gathers enthusiasts everywhere it is cultivated throughout the world.

About the fastest-growing of all vegetables, the radish develops from seed to edible bulb in 20 to 30 days when the weather is favorable. You can enjoy waves of edible bulbs all summer long by planting and replanting short rows repeatedly, every ten days or so. If hot weather should wipe out a crop or two (it makes them go all to tops) you haven't lost too much; just keep planting right through late summer.

While radishes will perform well in just about any area, they tend to develop too much top growth and stunted roots if planted too thickly, or in the shade, or in soil too high in nitrogen. Thinning is very important.

PLANT sparingly in rows 1-2 feet apart at a ¼" depth. Firm soil well. Seedlings will appear in less than a week.

THIN relentlessly until plants are spaced about 1" apart in the rows.

SPECIAL RECOMMENDATIONS:
Radishes offer a variety of choices in
colors (red, white, bi-color, pink, black)
and shapes (globular, olive-shaped,
elliptical, icicle). Most of the
icicle-shaped varieties are slower to
mature, but last longer without
becoming pithy. You should also
consider the slow-maturing winter
types, which will keep in storage over
the late fall and winter. Radishes grow
best in cool soil with full sun, so plant
them as soon as the frost leaves the
ground. Sturdy, fast-growing radishes
make good "pilot plants" for
slower-growing, less vigorous
vegetables; many gardeners sow radish
seeds along with their carrots or
onions.

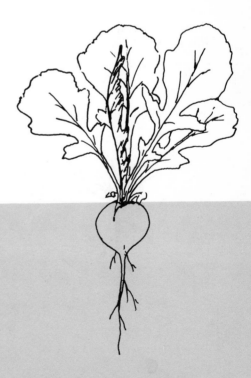

HARVEST while radishes are still crisp
and mild. If left in the ground too long
they will turn pithy and strong.

RHUBARB

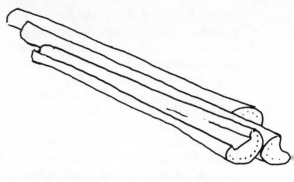

Here is another of the perennials that should be allotted its own area in your garden and then let alone. Once established, a stand of rhubarb (*Rheum rhaponticum*) will continue to bear for many years. It has long been a favorite for pies, sauces and cobblers, and also produces a delicious homemade white wine.

Rhubarb thrives where winters are cold, and it comes up early in the spring. During World War II, Russia faced a nutritional crisis when Hitler's armies overran the fruit-growing areas of the Crimea and southern U.S.S.R. which produced nearly all of her peaches, pears, apricots, cherries, apples, etc. Left with only their northern areas, in which most fruits would not grow, the resourceful Russians bought tons of rhubarb seed from the United States and embarked on a rhubarb-growing campaign that eventually provided them with plenty of this acid "fruit."

Rhubarb finds its way into many flower gardens because of its tall, broad-leaved beauty and interesting pink-tinged coloration.

Don't expect much in the way of a harvest for a year or two after you make your first planting, even if you use divisions or crowns. Seed-grown rhubarb will take even longer. Premature harvesting can adversely affect later crops.

SEED-PROPAGATED: Plant seeds in either spring or fall, sowing sparingly in rows 4 to 6 feet apart. Seedlings will appear in 12 to 14 days.

PLANT-PROPAGATED: Set out divisions or crowns every 3 feet or so in rows 5 feet apart.

SPECIAL RECOMMENDATIONS: Use
only the stalks of rhubarb; the leaves
are mildly poisonous. About two plants
per person will be adequate unless you
plan considerable freezing or canning.
Rhubarb can be planted in either sun or
shade.

FREEZING: Remove leaves and woody
ends; wash thoroughly and cut into
1-inch lengths. Do not blanch. For
short-term storage (3-4 months) just
package and freeze. For use as sauce,
cover with sugar syrup (3½ cups sugar
to 1 qu. cold water) and freeze. For pie
filling, add 1 cup sugar for each 4 cups
rhubarb and freeze.

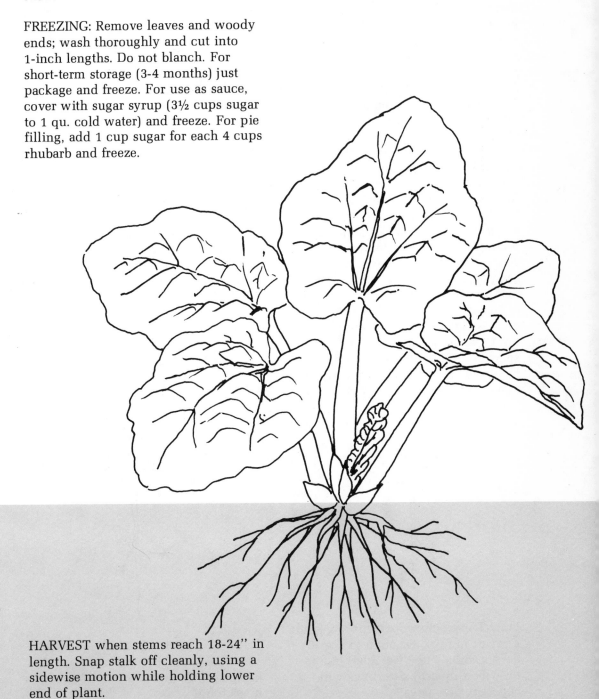

HARVEST when stems reach 18-24'' in
length. Snap stalk off cleanly, using a
sidewise motion while holding lower
end of plant.

❧ SQUASH ❧

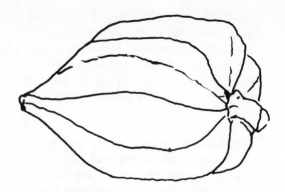

You're probably already familiar with the taste of home-grown squash; this vegetable produces so prolifically that harvest time finds most gardeners giving away quantities of it to their friends and neighbors.

There are two main types, both native to the Western Hemisphere. Summer squash (*Cucurbita pepo*) is harvested in its early immature state in midsummer, before the seeds and rind have begun to harden. The entire fruit is eaten — diced, sliced, sauteed or in casserole. Or you can just boil it in its own juices with no water. There are a number of varieties (Zucchini, Early Crookneck, Straightneck, Bush Scallop, etc.) all fast-growing and continuous-bearing. If you take the trouble to keep your summer squash picked, you will enjoy a steady harvest of dinner treats right up until frost.

The other type, called winter squash (*C. moschata* and *C. maxima* plus a few *C. pepo*) is harvested later in the summer or fall, after the rind has hardened and the flesh has matured into a deep yellow or orange color.

Only the flesh of winter squash is eaten; it is sweet, mealy and similar to yams or sweet potatoes. Usually it is served baked or steamed on the rind. Winter squash is the type to plant for winter storage.

SPECIAL RECOMMENDATIONS: Wait until a week or two after last average frost date to plant; squash doesn't have much cold resistance. Summer squash has the best flavor at 4-6" in length. Pick winter squash with part of the stem on, and avoid bruising. Two

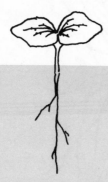

PLANT in a sunny spot, spacing seeds 4" apart in rows. Or put 6 to 8 seeds 1" deep in hills 4 to 6 feet apart (6-8 feet for winter squash). Seedlings will appear in 6-10 days.

THIN rows gradually until you have one vigorous plant every 3-4 feet. Thin hill plantings to the best 3 or 4 plants in each hill.

plants of summer squash or four of winter squash will supply one person adequately.

FREEZING: Blanch 1" slices of summer squash for 2-3 minutes, then chill in cold water, drain and freeze. Cut winter squash into large pieces, remove seeds and bake or steam until tender. Scoop and mash pulp, then cool and freeze. CANNING: Steam or bake large pieces (winter squash preferred) after removing seeds. Scoop and rice the pulp, add boiling water to make consistency a little thinner than pie mix. Can in usual way.

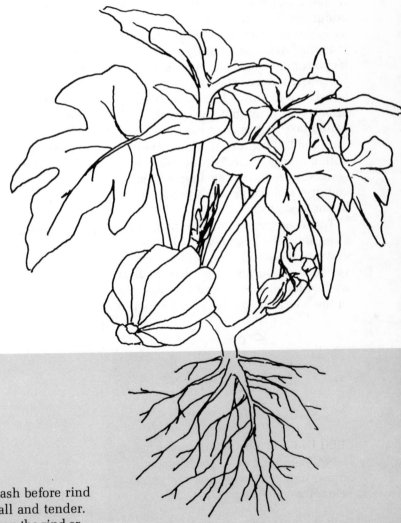

HARVEST summer squash before rind hardens, while still small and tender. Winter squash is ripe when the rind or skin is hard to the fingernail.

TOMATOES

Far and away the most popular crop of the home gardener, the tomato (*Lycopersicon esculentum*) hasn't had it easy in achieving its present universal acceptance. Believe it or not, at one time most Americans thought it was poisonous. The tomato originated somewhere in the Peru-Ecuador-Bolivia area and was cultivated as food by the Indians. European explorers brought tomato plants back to their homelands; in Italy the "poma d'oro," as they call it, has been grown and eaten since the middle of the 16th century. But somehow, perhaps because the tomato is in the Nightshade family, which has its poisonous members, Americans became convinced the tomato was lethal. It was grown here as an ornamental plant, but few people would take a chance on eating it. Not until the last century was this strange notion finally dispelled (probably by amused Europeans traveling in this country) and the tomato's popularity began to skyrocket.

Tomatoes come in a wide range of sizes, from the huge Beefsteak type down to the small pear, plum or cherry varieties measuring only a half-inch or so. Red tomatoes are most popular, but in the South the pink-skinned varieties are often preferred. Yellow varieties are often used to provide a pleasing accent on a salad plate.

SPECIAL RECOMMENDATIONS: Shallow hoeing is best for tomatoes. Don't overwater them; this can result in cracked fruit or can even kill the plant by keeping oxygen away from the roots. If you buy your transplants, avoid leggy or off-colored plants; this indicates crowding or nutritional deficiencies. Plant 3 to 4 plants per person, more for canning or juice-making.

SEED IN FLATS about six weeks before last average frost date. Seedlings will appear in 6 to 10 days. Harden plants before transplanting.

MOVE SEEDLINGS OUTDOORS when all frost danger is past. Choose a sunny location. Set transplants every 3 to 4 feet (or thin direct-seeded plants to that spacing) and don't forget cutworm precautions.

TOMATO JUICE: Just boil tomatoes in their own juice for a few minutes, run through a food mill to remove seeds and skin, add salt and sugar to taste. This produces a memorable tomato juice with fresh-from-the-garden flavor.

FREEZING: Results are spotty with frozen tomatoes. They usually thaw to a mushy state and skins are tough. Many homemakers find they add a fresh tomato flavor to soups, stews and casseroles, however. Just wrap whole tomatoes and freeze. Use them within 3 months or so.

HARVEST mature fruit on a regular basis; this tends to stimulate more production and eliminates unsightly rotting.

MORE ON TOMATOES

CAGING. This is a comparatively new technique for supporting tomato plants. Take a 5-foot length of heavy 6x6'' wire mesh (of the type used to reinforce concrete) and form it into a cylinder. Push this cylinder into the ground (snip off the bottom rung for extra penetrating depth). You now have a simple, neat support that reportedly increases the percentage of perfect fruit — the plant grows through the openings in the wire, which supports and protects it without the need for tying up new stems as they form. There is also less ground rot and rodent damage.

TEPEES. Lash a few 1x1'' stakes together tepee-fashion and you have a workable support for a number of tomato plants. Don't forget the horizontal slats.

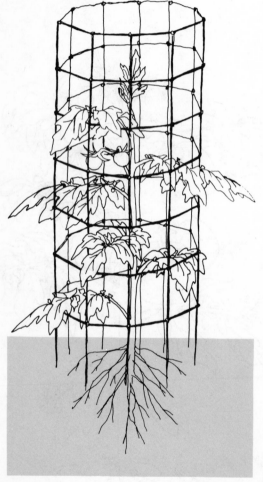

PICK OFF SUCKERS. (Only recommended with staked tomatoes.) It's a good idea to pinch off suckers when they're 3'' or so in size (a sucker is a shoot that grows in the axils or V's formed by stems off the main stalk).

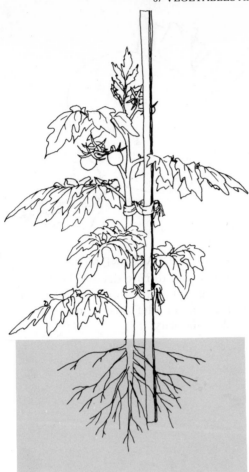

OTHER AILMENTS: *Leaf roll* is a condition in which some lower leaves form a stiff, tight roll. Fruiting is unaffected by this.

Chemical injury can be caused by drift from lawn or garden herbicides from as far as a half-mile away. Tomato plants are very sensitive to tiny traces of chemicals.

Blossom-end rot is a common ailment of tomatoes — a dry, leathery rotting on the fruit usually caused by moisture fluctuations.

HOW TO STAKE TOMATOES: Simply drive a 7-foot stake deep enough for firm support and tie the plant to it (use cloth strips to avoid cutting the plant). Tomatoes grown on supports are cleaner and easier to pick, but yield is decreased somewhat and you may have more cracked or sunscalded fruit.

LAST HARVEST. Just before the first freeze in the fall, pick all your tomatoes — red, pink, green. Wrap the immature ones in paper and store them in the dark at about 55°F. They will gradually ripen to provide you with fresh tomatoes over a period of several weeks. Or use them green in pickles, relishes, spreads or catsup.

BLOSSOM DROP. Sometimes tomatoes will fail to set fruit after blossoming; the flowers just drop off. This can be caused by too-hot weather (95°F or more) or a cool spell (55°F or less) at the time pollination should be taking place. You can aid matters by shaking the plant now and then after it blossoms; this causes pollen grains to drop from the plant's anthers to the stigma and makes pollination more likely.

❧ TURNIPS ☙

A staple food through the centuries for both man and beast, the turnip (*Brassica rapa*) supplies flavorsome roots that can be boiled or baked, plus nutritious leaves that are rich in vitamins and minerals. Turnips were first raised on this continent when Cartier introduced them into Canada during the reign of Henry VIII; they subsequently became popular with both colonists and Indians. Turnips are now more generally planted in the South than elsewhere. They are delicious when harvested fairly young; simply boil or steam, and serve with butter, salt and pepper.

One of the fastest-maturing and easiest to grow of all vegetables, the turnip is very hardy and does best at cool temperatures. Many gardeners plant a crop in late summer or even early fall; turnips can be left in the ground to mature until freeze-up with no damage.

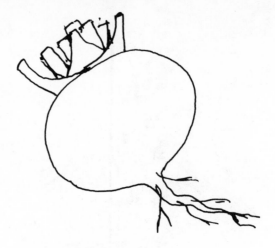

SPECIAL RECOMMENDATIONS: Keep well watered during dry spells. Turnips taste best when they grow quickly, so fertilize them after final thinning to hasten maturity.

PLANT as soon as frost leaves the ground in the spring, placing seeds ½" deep in rows 1 to 2 feet apart. Firm soil well and begin cultivation as soon as seedlings appear (4-7 days).

THIN gradually when plants are 3" high, until they are 3-4" apart. (No thinning is necessary if you are raising turnips for their greens, which will be ready for eating after a month or so.)

FREEZING: Remove tops from tender young turnips. Wash, peel and slice or dice into ½" pieces. Blanch in water 2½ minutes, chill in cold water, drain and freeze immediately. CANNING: Prepare as for freezing, then boil 3 minutes and can. (Turnips often become discolored and develop a strong flavor when canned.)

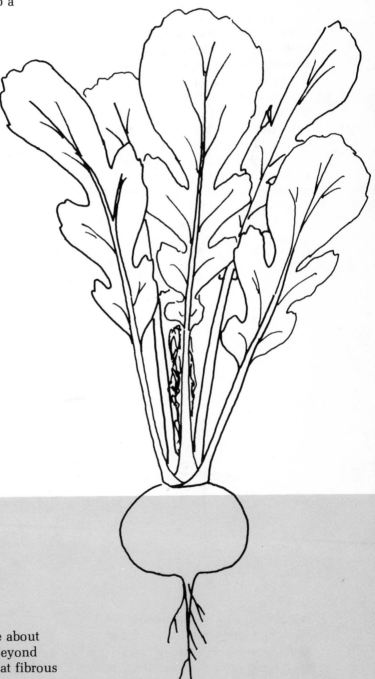

HARVEST roots when they are about 2" in diameter for best taste. Beyond that size they become somewhat fibrous and strong-flavored.

WATERMELON

A familiar crop since prehistoric times, the watermelon (*Citrullus vulgaris*) was originally believed to be native to Asia, although no specimens could be found growing wild there. Central Africa was finally established as its place of origin when England's famous explorer Dr. David Livingstone discovered great quantities growing wild in that area. Watermelon has become increasingly popular with home gardeners since the development of new short-season varieties that produce tasty fruit even in northern latitudes. Sweet-flavored small varieties are also available, weighing from 7 to 10 pounds.

Watermelons require plenty of growing space and there is no way to beat the space problem, since the fruit must lie on the ground. They do best in sandy loam soil that gets plenty of sunshine over a long growing season. Fertilize carefully if at all — too much nitrogen in the soil will result in luxuriant foliage and very few fruit.

PLANT after all frost danger is past. Put 6 to 8 seeds in hills 6 to 8 feet apart, or every 4 inches in rows 6 feet apart. Firm an inch of soil over each and look for seedlings in 8 to 12 days.

THIN to the best 2 or 3 plants in each hill, or to a 2-foot spacing in the rows.

HARVESTING TIPS: One of the major perplexities of beginning gardeners is how to tell when a watermelon is ripe. There is no lack of suggested methods, particularly those that advise you to thump, press or rap the ripening fruit. But the most reliable indicators are the visual ones:

• With most melons, blackening and shriveling of the tendril nearest the fruit indicates that the melon is ripe.

• Ripe melons lose their powdery or slick appearance, and become somewhat dull and rough-surfaced.

• Ripe melons turn yellowish-brown on the bottom surface. (This is probably the best indicator, although a very few melons have white bottoms when ripe.)

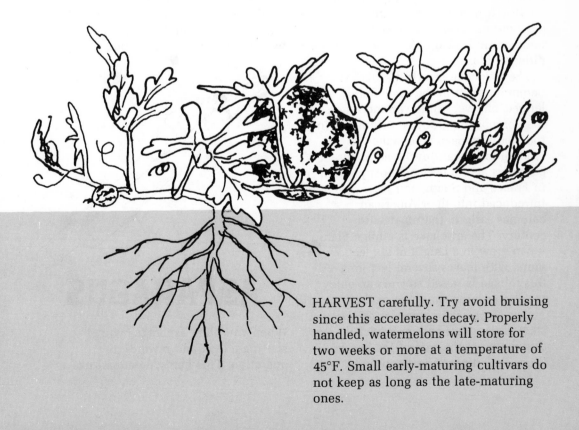

HARVEST carefully. Try avoid bruising since this accelerates decay. Properly handled, watermelons will store for two weeks or more at a temperature of 45°F. Small early-maturing cultivars do not keep as long as the late-maturing ones.

MORE POSSIBILITIES:

ARTICHOKE

The artichoke we will discuss is the Globe Artichoke (*Cynara scolymus*) often served in salads or as a hot accompaniment to meat dishes. Don't confuse it with the Jerusalem Artichoke (*Helianthus tuberosus*) raised for its underground tubers; this is a totally different plant.

The artichoke is a thistle-like perennial plant in the same family as lettuce, endive, sunflower and others of the *Compositae* group. It originated in the Mediterranean area, where its modern form was developed many centuries ago. It became most popular in France and Spain, and was introduced into their American colonies early in the nineteenth century. The artichoke is a huge plant; it can grow to a height of six feet or more, with leaves several feet long. All this foliage is raised so you can enjoy the flower buds, only two or three inches across, which appear on the stem of the plant and on branches originating at the base of the leaves. Since the artichoke is a perennial, you

should plant it in a part of your garden where it will remain undisturbed for several years. With ideal growing conditions, artichokes will produce flower buds the first year; normally they will then keep producing for three or four years, after which it's a good idea to replace them with fresh plants. Artichokes are extremely sensitive to frost; if you live in a cold climate, be sure to find out whether artichokes can be successfully grown in your area. In some cases a heavy covering of mulch will enable the plants to survive the winter; in others it may be necessary to grow the plants in large boxes or cases that can be moved indoors during the cold months. Best crops of edible buds usually occur when the spring weather is on the cool side; premature hot spells can cause too-rapid development and a tough texture in the buds.

SOW indoors 6 weeks before the last frost is expected, and move outside (or plant divisions) when weather permits. HARVEST when buds are not more than 4" in diameter, cutting an inch or two below the base of the bud.

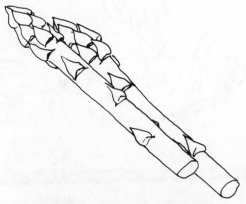

ASPARAGUS

When you plant asparagus you're starting a long and rewarding operation. This hardy perennial has a root system that increases in size and numbers each year if it is properly maintained; there are records of asparagus beds producing tasty spears for a century or more. However, you can't expect much production for quite a while, even if you plant crowns (well-established plants) in the first place. You will be able to cut fresh spears from the second season on, but it will be some time (3-4 years from seed) before the bed is producing in quantity.

If you're short of gardening space, there's no reason why you can't intercrop between the asparagus rows during the time you're waiting for the bed to come into production. Plantings of lettuce, beans or carrots will not disturb the development of the asparagus.

Asparagus likes deep, loose soil, so be sure to prepare the bed well. Remember that once your asparagus bed is in place, you will probably not disturb it for many years.

Asparagus grows wild in the eastern Mediterranean area, where it is believed to have originated, and references to it appear in many ancient writings. Asparagus was believed at one time to be a cure for a number of ailments from heart trouble to toothache.

Edible spears appear as soon as warm spring weather arrives. Harvest and enjoy! Be sure to keep spears cut when 8-10" high and before tips of spears expand. Can or freeze any excess. By midsummer or earlier, cease cutting and allow shoots to grow and vegetate. This furnishes roots with the store of food they need for the following year's production.

SET CROWNS in the bottom of 12"-wide trenches dug 10" deep, positioning tops about 6" below top of trench. Space about a foot apart and cover with 2" of soil. Water well.

HARVEST by cutting off at ground level or below.

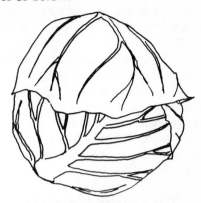

CABBAGE

A popular and highly nutritious vegetable that can be grown practically anywhere there is fertile, moist soil, cabbage (*Brassica oleracea*, var. *capitata* Linn.) offers a pleasant surprise to gardeners accustomed to the somewhat strong flavor of supermarket cabbage. Fast growth should be encouraged with liberal applications of fertilizer and regular watering; cabbage responds quickly to favorable growing conditions.

Its major drawback is a tendency toward disease problems and insect infestation. Choose disease-resistant varieties where possible, and check often for invasions of aphids, cabbage worms and root maggots.

There are many interesting cabbage varieties for the home gardener to try. The Savoy types have a crinkled, rumpled head and a flavor somewhat milder than other cabbages. Red cabbage gives a pleasing color accent to salads and is a major component of many hearty German dishes. Chinese cabbage, which is a different species entirely, comes in both chunky and long tubular shapes, with a mild, delicious flavor. Chinese cabbage has a tendency to bolt in hot weather, so most people grow it in late summer or fall.

Except in mild areas, most cabbage is grown from well-started plants that are either propagated via the transplant method (see page 34) or purchased at garden stores. The latter are often sturdy plants grown over the winter in southern areas; these are usually hardier than northern-grown transplants. A light purple cast on the leaves indicates that they have been hardened off well.

PLANT at two-foot spacing, firming the soil well around the roots. HARVEST when heads are well formed and firm to the touch.

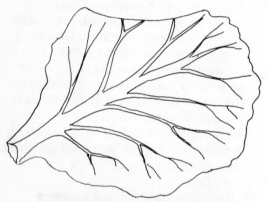

COLLARDS

These are leafy non-heading cabbages (*Brassica oleracea* var. *acephala*) that are rich in minerals and vitamins. One of the easiest vegetables to grow, collards supply winter greens in home gardens throughout the South, but develop a strong flavor if raised in very hot weather.

Collards are believed to be one of the primitive cabbage forms. They were well known by the ancient Romans, who probably introduced them into conquered France and Britain, from where colonists brought them to this country.

PLANT in spring for early harvest, in midsummer for fall or winter crop. Sow seeds 1" apart, firm ½" of soil over them. HARVEST only tender young leaves; avoid disturbing older leaves and central growing part of the plant.

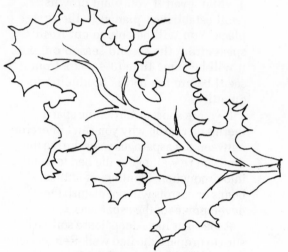

ENDIVE

The slight bitterness of endive (*Cichorium endivia*) has limited its popularity somewhat in this country, but it has long been a favorite in Europe. The ancient Egyptians, Greeks and Romans praised it often, and it has been a staple in northern Europe for centuries. There are two types: *Curly endive* has narrow, ragged-edge outer leaves that are somewhat bitter, but its inner leaves are yellowish-white and very tasty. *Batavian endive* (or *escarole*) has broader, thicker leaves and delicious heart leaves that blanch to a creamy white. The latter type tolerates slight shade well. Endive keeps producing all summer if kept picked (or cut). Unlike lettuce, it can experience hot weather without bolting or becoming inedible.

SOW in early spring at ¼" depth in rows 2-3' apart. Thin to 6-8" spacing.

HARVEST at will. (Tie maturing outer leaves together loosely to blanch inner leaves for extra flavor.)

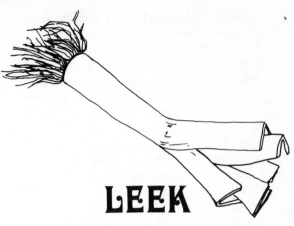

LEEK

You'll probably like leeks (*Allium porrum*) for their distinctive flavor — milder than an onion — but the Emperor Nero was convinced that eating leeks improved his singing voice, and he consumed quantities of them. Leeks can be difficult to raise — they need about 14 weeks of fairly constant mild weather from seeding to maturity — but they are quite popular with home gardeners, particularly those who dislike the strong flavor of other members of the onion family.

In general, their cultivation is similar to that suggested for onions.

KOHLRABI

Often described as an "above-ground turnip," kohlrabi has a mild, sweet flavor with overtones of both turnip and cabbage. Its crisp texture makes it an interesting addition to stews and casseroles, or you can serve it raw as part of a relish tray. Thin slices sauteed in butter are also delicious.

Kohlrabi is one of the few vegetables that can tolerate moderate shade. It grows so quickly it is recommended for succession plantings. Kohlrabi should be harvested before it reaches its full size. Beyond 2" or so in diameter, it tends to develop woody fibers and a somewhat stronger taste.

PLANT as soon as the soil can be worked in the spring; kohlrabi does best with a long, cool growing season. In the south, plant as a fall or winter crop. Sow sparingly in rows 2 feet apart, and thin to 3-4" spacing. HARVEST at any time after stem has become bulbous.

PARSLEY

Every gardener should raise a bit of parsley for use as a garnish; it takes just a few plants to produce all the average family needs. And parsley adds a piquant flavor to many dishes, too. To the Greeks and Romans it was not only a food and decoration, but also wearing apparel — they used it often in their festive garlands because it kept its pleasing green color indefinitely. Just a sprig of parsley on a plate of meat or almost any dish adds a little beauty and elegance to the simplest serving.

Parsley is quite slow to sprout (18-24 days) so you may wish to soak seeds in warm water for 24 hours before planting as an aid to germination.

PLANT sparingly in rows 1½-2' apart. Press ¼" of soil over seeds. Thin to 4" apart. HARVEST at will; cut stems with a sharp knife and the plant will keep producing. In the fall, dig up one or two plants to keep in a sunny window for pinches of fresh parsley all winter (roots are deep, so use a deep container).

PUMPKIN

Every child makes the acquaintance of the pumpkin early in life; this traditional symbol of harvest time and Halloween is a source of fond recollections for all.

The pumpkin (*Cucurbita sp.*) is the biggest member of the squash family (see page 110 for growing instructions) and with special effort you can often

produce a specimen of gigantic size. Here's how to do it:

Choose one of the mammoth varieties. (Big Max, for instance). Follow the instructions for planting winter squash in hills, and select the hill with the most vigorous seedlings for special treatment. Pick off all but the one healthiest-looking plant in that hill, and give it good-sized feedings of fertilizer every week throughout the growing season. In early summer, as the fruits begin to set, pick off all but the one largest fruit on the plant you have selected. Continue the weekly fertilizing, and be sure the plant gets adequate water also. This entire flow of nutrients will go to that one remaining fruit, and you should be rewarded with a pumpkin of sizable proportions.

When it has reached maximum size, cut it off the vine, leaving a stem attached, and leave it in place for a few days until the skin has had time to harden. Then it is ready to be moved indoors.

Incidentally, for a delicious "pumpkin" pie, try making it out of winter squash (Buttercup, Butternut, Hubbard or similar varieties). You probably won't be able to tell the difference.

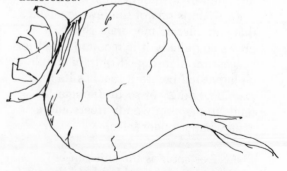

RUTABAGAS

Believed to be the result of a natural hybridization between turnip and cabbage, the rutabaga (*Brassica napobrassica)* is grown mostly in our northern states and in Canada, where it is known as the Swede turnip. It is also popular in Britain and the northern European countries. While the yellow-fleshed kind is most familiar, there are also white-fleshed varieties.

Vitamin-rich and robust-flavored, rutabagas are often served as an accompaniment to turkey or other poultry. A favorite Scandinavian dish is mashed potatoes and rutabagas — half and half — served with plenty of butter. *Deilig! Storslået! Jättebra!*

The rutabaga likes loose, sandy loam soil and does especially well on new land freshly brought into use. In northern long-day summers it develops enormous (5-6 pounds) and delicious roots by fall. It stores well in a cool place.

In some areas, root maggots will tunnel into rutabaga roots unless a proper soil insecticide is applied.

PLANT seeds ⅛" deep in rows 3' apart. Thin to an 8" spacing when plants are 3" tall. HARVEST in late fall when roots reach 4-6" in diameter. They can be left in the ground to mature until heavy frost.

packed with vitamins. It must have cool weather for best results; grow it quickly during the moderate temperatures of spring and early summer — it goes to seed quickly in hot weather. Because of this characteristic, many home gardeners prefer to plant chard, which withstands summer heat well and also lets you harvest leaves at will (spinach is harvested only once in most areas; the entire plant is cut off at ground level).

Another possible alternative is New Zealand spinach *(Tetragonia expansa)* which will survive considerable heat and continues bearing edible leaves throughout the season. It is delicious either cooked or raw.

Insects and disease may be problems in some areas; look for disease-resistant varieties when you buy spinach seed, and inspect your plants often for evidence of invasion by spinach aphids and leaf miners.

Fertilize and water well to encourage fast growth; this results in greener, more tender leaves.

PLANT as early in the spring as possible. Sow sparingly at ½" depth, and thin to 4-6" spacing when plants are 3-4" tall. HARVEST when leaves reach a good size and are still in rosette form, before terminal upright growth begins.

SPINACH

Grown practically everywhere in the world, spinach *(Spinacia oleracea)* is a fast-growing crop that produces large quantities of broad and tender leaves

HERBS

Part of the fun of planting an herb garden is the wealth of folklore, history and superstition it opens up to us. To most moderns, herbs are merely pretty rows of neatly labeled jars in someone's kitchen. But at one time herbs were grown by just about every householder as a source of medicinal salves, liniments and tinctures; of cosmetics, soporifics, breath fresheners and deodorants. The flowers were used for perfumes and wines; "strewing herbs" made fragrant carpets for homes, castles and theaters. Sprigs of different herbs acquired symbolic meanings and were used as messages of hope, sympathy, happiness, and just about every other human emotion. Herbs were even credited with supernatural and magical powers; they were used as good luck charms and proof against evil spirits.

With the development of modern medicine, drugstores, the greeting card industry and our ability to buy things rather than make them, much of the lore surrounding herbs has ceased to be passed from generation to generation. Few people are even aware of the extent to which the early colonists depended on herbs that they raised themselves or gathered near home. So necessary was this source of medicines, seasonings and perfumes that many a family included packets of seeds and cuttings of their favorite herbs in the baggage they brought to the New World.

Herbs are still widely used in many underdeveloped countries and today there's a reawakening of interest in them in America. Fortunately the literature on the subject is extensive and goes back for thousands of years.

Incidentally, we're using the word "herb" in its popular sense, meaning a special group of plants grown for their delicate flavors or scents, or perhaps for some mild medicinal purpose.

Botanists, however, define an herb as a plant without a permanent woody stem, which would include just about all the world's plants except trees and shrubs. And would exclude such favorites as rosemary and sage, which develop woody stems.

WHERE TO PLANT

It makes sense to place your herb garden as close to the kitchen door as possible. This makes it easy for the cook to snip off fragrant sprigs as they are needed. Also, of course, it simplifies watering and cultivating.

Another popular spot is in border plantings, along walks and driveways. The colorful, oddly patterned foliage of herbs adds an interesting note to any garden arrangement, and this usually lasts throughout the season — sometimes even beyond killing frosts. Several kinds of herbs give off a delightful fragrance, and many produce flowers of singular beauty.

In choosing a spot for your herbs, try to avoid windy locations. A sheltered, sunny spot is best. Plant a protective border of shrubs if necessary; this will temper the wind without cutting down air circulation excessively.

As a rule, pests and diseases are not much of a problem with herbs. In fact, many herbals recommend planting certain herbs in the vegetable garden as insect repellents. However, keep in mind that some herbs (such as borage or bergamot) have an irresistible attraction for bees.

WHAT TO PLANT

Among the culinary herbs popular with home gardeners are anise, balm, basil, borage, caraway, chervil, chives, dill, fennel, hyssop, marjoram, mint, parsley, rosemary, sage, savory, tarragon and thyme.

A number of others are favorites because of their aromatic foliage, including lavender, rue, bergamot, basil, thyme and rosemary.

While few herbs are actually raised by home gardeners for their medicinal qualities nowadays, there are quite a number of this type: foxglove (source of digitalis), aloe (the first-aid plant), henbane, licorice, tansy, wormwood, red poppy, pennyroyal, chamomile and others.

HOW TO PLANT

Most herbs are started from seed, except for tarragon, mint, and a few others which must be bought as plants. The slow growers, such as lavender and rosemary, are often given a head start also, either by using well-started plants or cuttings. Many of the seed-propagated herbs are of this nature, slow and erratic to germinate, so be patient.

Since the quantity you will need of any herb is quite small, you may wish to plant your herbs in boxes or barrels. This has several advantages: you can vary soil content easily to suit individual species; you can move the containers if necessary to fill particular needs for sunshine and rainfall; you can bring cold-sensitive herbs inside over the winter.

In general, planting and cultivating procedures for herbs are the same as those for vegetables; just follow the packet instructions. Well-drained soil is a must for most herbs, however.

HARVESTING AND DRYING

You can cut fresh sprigs of most herbs (parsley, thyme, sage, marjoram, etc.) with no damage to the plants. Herbs to be dried and stored are usually cut just as they are ready to bloom. They can be dried slowly in a warm oven or on racks in an airy room. Or you can dry them in paper bags hung from rafters. When leaves are totally dry (they should fall away from the stems and powder easily), crush or grind them and store in airtight containers. Small stoppered jars are excellent.

Herbs grown for their seeds (caraway, dill, etc.) should be harvested just before the seeds drop of their own accord. Blanch them in boiling water to kill any insects, and put them in paper bags to dry.

If you have freezer space available, this is the most convenient way of keeping herbs. Store them in stapled sandwich bags, but keep portions small — herbs can't be refrozen.

In time most dried herbs will gradually lose flavor. After a year or so you might want to check your dried herbs, replacing any that have lost their essence.

HOW TO USE HERBS

Many cooking secrets are locked up in the subtle flavors of different herbs. Inventive cooks find them invaluable for adding fresh interest to standard dishes and creating new delights for the dinner table. It is a skill that is learned slowly, however. Herbs are at their best in bringing out the inherent flavor of the dishes themselves, rather than superimposing flavors of their own. The knack lies in adding just the right amount of the right herb to each

dish. The best approach is to start with just a hint, and gradually increase the amount used. (There's a saying that if you can taste the herb in a dish, you've used too much.)

Herb use varies with individual taste and is greatly influenced by ethnic and cultural customs. There is also considerable variation in the strength of different herbs, depending on whether they are used fresh or dried, the amount of sunshine they received while growing, plus soil conditions, moisture levels and other factors. Your home-grown herbs will usually have much more flavoring power than the commercial mixtures you may be accustomed to.

POPULAR HERBS

This is by no means a complete list; you will probably want to investigate many other possibilities. Herb gardeners are a congenial lot, and eager to try new varieties. Since it takes very few plants of any herb to supply normal needs, you will probably find yourself eventually with surplus plants. It's fun to exchange these for varieties you lack; the number of herbs you can try is almost unlimited.

Herb	Botanical Name	Annual-A Perennial-P Biennial-B	Height	Plant Spacing	How Propagated	Parts Used	Usage
Anise	Pimpinella anisum	A	1½-2'	8-10"	seeds	leaves, seeds	cakes, cookies, liqueurs
Angelica	Angelica archangelica	P	5-6'	24"	seeds division	leaves	salads, flavoring
Balm	Melissa officinalis	P	2'	12"	seeds	leaves	cold drinks, teas, liqueurs
Basil	Ocimum basilicum	A	1½-2'	10"	seeds	leaves	soups, stews, omelets, salads, egg dishes
Bergamot	Monarda didyma	P	3'	15"	seeds division	leaves	tea
Borage	Borago officinalis	A	1½-2'	10"	seeds	leaves	garnish in salads, drinks
Caraway	Carum carvi	B	1½-2'	12"	seeds	seeds	breads, cakes, confections, soups, liqueurs
Catnip	Nepeta cataria	P	2-3'	12"	seeds division	leaves, shoots	bee plant, attractive to cats
Chervil	Anthriscus cerefolium	A	1-1½'	10"	seeds	leaves	garnish, soups, salads
Chives	Allium schoeniprasum	P	1'	12"	seeds division	leaves	ornamental, hot bread, omelets, cottage cheese
Coriander	Coriandrum sativum	A	2-2½'	15"	seeds	seeds	cakes, cookies, confections, curries, drinks
Dill	Anethum graveolens	A	2'	12"	seeds	seed clusters	pickles, salads, fish, sauerkraut
Fennel (Sweet)	Foeniculum officinale	A&P	3½-4'	18-24"	seeds	leaves, shoots	salads, soups, fish, bread, confections, vinegar
Horehound	Marrubium vulgare	P	1½-3'	10"	seeds division	oil from leaves	candy, lozenges
Hyssop	Hyssopus officinalis	P	1½-2'	10"	seeds and division	leaves	egg dishes, salads, teas, condiments, perfume
Lavender	Lavandula spica	P	2'	12"	seeds and division	leaves	sachets, linens, perfumes
Lemon Balm	Melissa officinalis	P	1½-2'	10"	root division	leaves	lemon flavoring
Lemon Verbena	Lippia citriadora	P	3'	15"	cuttings	leaves	jellies, sachets, pot pourri
Marjoram	Origanum marjorana	P	1½-2'	6"	seeds and division	leaves	salads, egg dishes, soups, dressings
Mint (many kinds)	Metha SP	P	2-3'	12"	divisions	leaves	cold drinks, teas
Parsley	Petroselinum hortense	B	2-3'	6"	seed	leaves	garnish, salads, potatoes, meat
Pennyroyal	Mentha pulegium	P	1-1½'	6"	seeds and division	leaves	extracts, medicines
Rosemary	Rosmarinus officinalis	P	2-3'	12"	seeds and division	leaves	meats, soups, stews, pickles, sauces
Rose geranium	Pelarganium graveolens	P	2'	15"	cuttings	leaves	jellies, sachets, pot pourri
Rue	ruta graveolens	P	1½-2'	10"	seeds and divisions	leaves	vinegar, salads
Saffron	Carthanimus, tinctaria	A	1½-2'	12"	seeds	blossoms	food coloring, dye
Sage	Salvia officinalis	P	12-15"	12"	seeds divisions	leaves	dressings, meats, gravies, tea, cheese
Summer Savory	Satureia hortensis	A	1½'	8"	seeds	leaves, shoots	dressings, salads, soups, teas, rice & bean dishes
Tarragon	Artemisia dracunculus	P	1½-2'	10"	division	leaves, shoots	vinegar, sauces, dressings
Thyme	Thymus vulgaris	P	8-12"	6"	seeds divisions	leaves	soups, dressings, salads, omelets, gravies, cheese
Wormwood	Artemisia absinthium	P	2-3'	10"	seeds division	leaves	tonics, vermifuge, liquors

GLOSSARY

ACCLIMATIZATION. Getting a plant used to strange new surroundings so it will survive and propagate.

ACIDITY. See "pH" in general index.

ADVENTITIOUS BUD. A bud that forms in an unexpected place on the plant — on a stalk, for instance, usually under conditions of stress.

AERATION. Keeping the soil's ventilating spaces open and functioning. This is usually done by Nature as rainwater carves tubes in the soil through which air then circulates. Earthworms and other beneficial tunneling organisms also do their part, as do freezing and thawing.

AEROBIC BACTERIA. These are bacteria that can function only when supplied with oxygen.

ALKALINITY. See "pH" in general index.

ALTERNATE HOST. One of two kinds of plants upon which a certain parasitic fungus must develop to complete its life cycle. The fungus develops spores on the first type of plant, which are then transported to a different type of plant (or alternate host) where their development is completed. Disease spores from the second plant are, in turn, carried back to the original host plant to keep the cycle going.

AMMONIUM NITRATE. Fertilizer with high nitrogen content (about 1/3 of its weight) which should be used carefully — it may burn foliage — and stored carefully, since it may be explosive under certain conditions.

AMMONIUM SULFATE. Fertilizer with lower (about 2%) nitrogen and high sulfur content, useful in acidifying soils with high pH level.

ANAEROBIC BACTERIA. Bacteria that can survive and work only without plentiful or free oxygen.

ANTHRACNOSE. Fungas-causing diseases that produce dead areas on plants. Is most likely to occur — or be spread — in wet weather.

AVAILABLE. As used by gardeners in connection with plant nutrients, this means that the food is in a form a plant can use. In most chemical fertilizers the nutrients are immediately available; natural fertilizers gradually decay and become available slowly.

BINOMIAL. The two-word botanical name of a plant, with the genus first, followed by the species (i.e. *Brassica oleracea* for broccoli).

BIOLOGICAL CONTROL. This is an adjunct of organic gardening by which harmful insects and other pests are controlled without the use of chemicals. Natural enemies, sterilized males, insect parasites, sex attractants, and other devices are employed to keep the pest population down.

BLANCHING. Process of whitening the

133

leaves or stems of certain plants by excluding light while they are growing.

BLASTING. A sudden plant failure in the budding, flowering or fruiting stage, usually caused by disease or unfavorable growing conditions.

BLIGHT. Diseases that cause sudden spotting, wilting or death of plants.

BOLTING. Sudden, untimely production of flowers or seed caused by a plant reacting to drought, excess heat or lack of nutrients. Also the second-year growth (flowering) of a biennial.

BULBIL. Small bulb produced in the flower heads by some onion types.

CHELATE. Term designating the molecular form in which some nutrients, usually iron or trace elements, become more easily absorbable by plants.

CHLOROSIS. Yellowing of foliage caused by a lack of chlorophyll. This is usually induced by a minerals deficiency, excessive soil alkalinity, or lack of moisture.

CLAY SOIL. Fine-particled soil that holds moisture tenaciously and takes a long time to dry out.

CLIMATE. Normal conditions of temperature, moisture, wind and other natural elements usually found in a particular area. In other words, long-term, year-to-year weather conditions.

CLOCHE. Bell-shaped protective cover for seedlings or out-of-season plants.

CLONING. Propagation of plants by tubers, slips, grafting or budding rather than from seed.

COTYLEDON. Embryonic seed leaf usually containing stored food for initial seedling growth.

COVER CROP. A fast-growing crop (such as ryegrass) that is turned under in the fall as a soil conditioner. Also known as a green manure crop.

CROWN. Growing point above root where tops originate.

CRUCIFER. A member of the mustard family (radish, turnip, cabbage, etc.), all of which have four-petaled cross-shaped flowers.

CUCURBIT. Any member of the gourd family (pumpkin, squash, cucumber, melon, etc.).

CULTIVAR. A cultivated variety, developed by plant breeding or selection, which differs from its original botanical species.

CULTIVATION. In the broad sense, managing the soil to give plants the most favorable environment for growth. Includes plowing, tilling, raking, hoeing, fertilizing, watering, aerating, etc.

DAY-NEUTRAL. Term for plant not influenced in its development by the comparative length of night and day.

DETERMINATE. Term for plants whose terminal growth stops when a flower bud is produced, such as some of the self-topping tomatoes, e.g. New Yorker.

DIATOMACEOUS EARTH. Mined whitish powder with insecticidal properties. It is inert chemically and kills insects by abrasive mechanical action.

DIBBER. Pointed tool for making holes in soft soil to accommodate transplants. Also called a dibble.

DICOTYLEDON. Large class of the plant kingdom in which the germinating seed produces two leaves initially. Includes most of the flowering and fruiting plants that we know.

DIOECIOUS. Term for plant having the male sex element (stamen) on one plant, the female element (pistil) on another.

DIVISION. Method of propagating plants by which the parent is divided into several portions, each with some root structure.

DORMANCY. Rest period taken by plants, usually in the winter but sometimes during the growing season when unseasonable conditions of cold, drought or heat occur. Changing day length can trigger it in some plants.

DUST MULCH. Surface layer of finely cultivated soil that helps retain subsoil moisture by breaking up the wicking action that normally occurs.

EARLY. Used in describing a *plant variety*, this means one that matures fast. However, an early *crop* is one that you plant early in the season.

EMBRYO. The tiny rudimentary plant inside a seed. Most of the seed consists of nutrients intended to nourish the embryo during its germination while it is developing its own food-producing apparatus.

ENDOSPERM. The nutritive tissue in seeds on which the germinating plant feeds. Occurs abundantly only in seeds of monocotyledonous plants. See *Embryo*.

ENZYMES. Various natural regulator compounds present in plants in very small amounts. These vital substances influence germination, growth, ripening, and other life processes.

ESCAPE. A cultivated plant that now grows wild.

ETIOLATION. See *Blanching*.

FERTILIZER BURN. Damage caused by applying commercial fertilizer directly to foliage or roots.

FERTILIZER, COMMERCIAL. Fertilizer you buy rather than that produced by your compost heap or domestic animals.

FERTILIZER, COMPLETE. Fertilizer containing all three essential elements: nitrogen, phosphorus and potassium.

FERTILIZER, SLOW-RELEASE. Fertilizer that gradually dissolves, releasing its nutrients to the soil in regular amounts over a long period of time.

FILLER, FERTILIZER. Inert material added to fertilizer mixtures to permit even distribution, reduce moisture

uptake from the air during storage and decrease likelihood of fertilizer burn.

FLOCCULATE. To give very fine clay soils a more granular character through additions of lime, organic matter or other soil conditioners.

FOLIAR FEEDING. Spraying the foliage and stems of plants with certain types of liquid fertilizer which can be absorbed and transported throughout the plant.

FORCING. Encouraging early or out-of-season growth, flowering or fruiting of plants through use of heat, artificial light or other devices.

FROST, BLACK. Frost that blackens foliage without formation of ice crystals on plant surfaces. Usually occurs in windy, unsettled weather.

FROST, WHITE. Ice crystals on plants and other objects formed when dew freezes. Usually occurs on clear, still nights.

FRUIT. Botanically, this is the developed ovary of higher plants in which ripened ovules or seeds occur.

FUNGICIDE. Compound used to kill disease-causing fungi.

FUNGUS. A low form of plant life that lacks chlorophyll and is unable to manufacture its own food. It extracts its nutrients from plant or animal matter, both dead and living. Fungi are responsible for many plant diseases such as rusts, molds and mildews.

GAS INJURY. Non-germination, growth retardation, wilting or destruction of plants resulting from gas main leaks, car exhausts, smelter fumes, etc. (Tomatoes are particularly sensitive.)

GEOTROPISM. Direction of plant growth (stems upward, roots downward) relative to the force of gravity. See also *Phototropism*.

GREEN MANURE. See *Cover Crop*.

GYNOPHORE. The stalk which bears the pistils of a flower.

HARDINESS. The degree to which a given plant can withstand adverse winter temperatures or conditions without injury.

HARDPAN. Hard-packed layer of soil just below the topsoil which is impervious to plant roots and must be broken up for gardening success.

HEAVY SOIL. Term that refers to the consistency of the soil, and not its weight. Heavy soil is a dense clay that resists working. Granular, porous, sandy soil that's easy to work is called "light," but actually it weighs more than dry clay.

HERBACEOUS. As used by gardeners, this term means any plant that dies to the ground each winter.

HERBICIDE. Weed-killing compound.

HETEROSIS. The increased vigor that results from a hybridization or crossing of two lines or races within a species.

HETEROZYGOUS. Term used to describe a plant whose two parents have given it differing genes, with the result that it does not breed true.

HOMOZYGOUS. Term for plant having sets of genes that are identical. This type of plant will breed true.

HORMONES. These are the mysterious substances within plant tissue which activate various functions such as flowering, fruiting, dormancy, etc. Scientists are still unsure about how they originate and whether they circulate throughout the plant or are developed by each individual cell.

HOST. A plant on or in which a parasitic organism lives.

HYBRID, F_1 This is a first-generation hybrid of two dissimilar parents. The F stands for "filial" and the inferior number indicates that this is the first generation after the initial cross was made. Hybrid vigor is usually at its peak in this generation, and declines somewhat in the succeeding generations (F_2, F_3, F_4, etc.) All vegetable or flower varieties labeled "Hybrid" are F_1 hybrids; if otherwise, they must be so designated.

HYDROPONICS. Soilless gardening — growing plants in a nutrient solution rather than in ordinary garden soil.

HYPOCOTYL. That portion of the axis of the embryo in a seed that develops into the root system.

IMMUNITY. Total ability on the part of a plant to withstand disease, adverse climatic conditions or insect infestation. See also *Klendusity, Resistance, Tolerance.*

INDETERMINATE. Term used for a plant whose stems do not have a terminal bud that stops upward growth. See also *Determinate.*

INDICATOR PLANT. Plant whose presence in a given area is a tip-off about changes that may be occurring in the area's soil or climatic conditions.

INDIGENOUS. Word describing plants or plant diseases native to a certain area. The opposite is *exotic.*

INFLORESCENCE. Word used by botanists to indicate the entire floral structure of a plant — the manner in which it develops its flowers, and particularly the anatomical arrangement of its buds and blossoms.

INOCULATION. In gardening nomenclature, treatment of seed with bacteria that stimulate the development of nitrogen nodules on plant roots. Used most often with peas, beans and other legumes.

INSECTICIDE. Preparation used to kill insects.

INTUMESCENCE. Blister formed when plant cells absorb an excess of water after a dry period.

KLENDUSITY. Avoidance of disease by a susceptible plant variety through a happy circumstance of growth. For example, an early variety of cucumbers, even though susceptible to powdery mildew, avoids being infected because powdery mildew usually doesn't develop until late in the season.

LATENT. Used to describe buds that are undeveloped and may remain so in the absence of specific stimuli such as defoliation by frost or insect infestation.

LEACHING. In gardening usage, removal of mineral elements from the soil by the percolating action of rainwater.

LEAF MOLD. Decayed leaves, useful for improving the tilth and fertility of soil.

LEGGY. Descriptive of weak-stemmed, overly tall plants that have been given improper care, such as too much heat or nutrients, crowding or insufficient light.

LOAM. The ideal soil mixture for gardening, with a consistency that is somewhere between clay and sand.

LONG-DAY PLANT. One that blooms in late spring or summer, responding to the lengthened daylight at that time of the year. See *Photoperiodism, Short-Day Plant*.

MACRONUTRIENT. Nutrient that plants require in large amounts — nitrogen, phosphorus, potassium, carbon, oxygen, etc. See also *Micronutrient*.

MANURE. Animal and vegetable matter used as a soil conditioner. Americans usually apply this term to animal excrement.

MICROCLIMATE. A variation from the overall climate of an area caused by localized surface features — hills, prevailing winds, large bodies of water, etc.—that results in special growing conditions.

MICRONUTRIENT. Nutrient that plants require only in small amounts — copper, iron, boron, molybdenum, zinc, etc. See also *Macronutrient*.

MICROORGANISM. To a gardener, any of the billions of microscopic plants and animals that are constantly at work attacking plants to cause disease, or are in the soil breaking down dead plant and animal residue and creating humus.

MONOCOTYLEDON. Large class of the plant kingdom in which the germinating seed produces one leaf initially. Includes the grasses, lilies, etc.

MONOECIOUS. Type of plant that has both male and female sex organs in different flowers on the same plant.

MOSAIC. Descriptive of diseases, usually virus-caused, that result in uneven coloration of leaves.

MUTANT. Plant exhibiting a sudden change in heredity, with new characteristics that breed true. Also called a "sport".

NEMATODE. One of the hundreds of species of microscopic wormlike organisms that often attack plant roots, causing stunted or unhealthy growth.

NITROGEN FIXATION. The transformation of free nitrogen into nitrogen compounds that can be absorbed as food by plants. This is done naturally through bacterial decomposition, nitrogen nodules on plant roots (see *Inoculation*), or by lightning. The nitrogen in commercial fertilizers is fixed by chemical or electrical processes.

NODULES. Small rounded knobs which, on the roots of vegetables in the pea family, indicate the presence of nitrogen-fixing bacteria. See *Inoculation*.

NURSE CROP. Sturdy plants grown next to some that are less vigorous in order to protect them during their germination and early growth.

PARASITE. An organism that lives on and derives its sustenance from another organism.

PARTHENOCARPY. The development of fruit without fertilization of ovules. Some chemical fruit-setting sprays induce this.

PATHOGEN. Any organism capable of causing disease.

PEAT MOSS. Partially-decomposed plant life taken from bogs and used as a rooting medium, soil conditioner or mulch.

PEDICLE. Stalk or stem supporting a flower.

PERLITE. Volcanic inert material with the same uses as vermiculite.

PETIOLE. Stalk or stem of a leaf.

pH. Rating scale that indicates relative acidity/alkalinity level of soil. Scale runs from 0 to 14, with 7 as neutral reading. Test readings of less than 7 indicate acid soil, above 7 alkaline.

PHLOEM. Plant tissue by which nutrients are moved from leaves to roots. See *Vascular*.

PHOTOPERIODISM. The effect of varying daylight length on such plant functions as flowering and setting of seed. See *Long-Day, Short-Day Plant*.

PHOTOTROPISM. The influence of light on the direction the different parts of a plant tend to grow (stems toward light, roots away from light). See also *Geotropism*.

PINNATE. Type of leaf which has an arrangement of leaflets on both sides of the center petiole, like a feather.

PISTIL. The female sex organ of a seed plant. Consists of stigma, style and ovary.

PLANT KINGDOM. In descending order, plants are classified according to their Division, Class, Subclass, Order, Family, Genus, Species and Variety. Thus the niche occupied in the Plant Kingdom by Greencrop Beans, for instance, is the Spermatophyta Division, Angiospermae Class, Dicotyledones Subclass, Rosales Order, Leguminosae Family, Phaseolus Genus, Vulgaris Species, and Greencrop Variety.

PLUMULE. The first bud of a plant when a seed germinates. In other words, the embryonic leaf structure.

POLLINATION, OPEN. This is natural, uncontrolled pollination with no interference by man.

POLLINATION, SELF. This is pollination of an individual plant with its own pollen.

POT-BOUND. Descriptive of a potted plant whose roots fill the pot almost entirely.

POTHERB. Any plant you raise for its greens.

POTTING MIXTURE. A combination of soil and other rooting media (peat, sand, perlite, vermiculite) designed to give transplants or indoor plants ideal surroundings for growth.

PRICKING-OFF. Colloquial term gardeners use for the process of transplanting new seedlings to larger flats or individual pots to give them more growing space.

PUDDLING. Dipping roots of transplants into a slurry made of soil and water. Helps prevent roots from drying out during transplanting process. Also refers to destruction of soil structure by working it when wet.

PUSTULE. A pimple-like growth usually indicative of plant disease.

RACE. A line of cultivated plants within a species and variety that can be expected to breed fairly true from seed. See *Homozygous*.

RADICLE. The first (or embryonic) root that develops from the lower portion of the hypocotyl of a sprouting seed.

RESISTANCE. Partial ability of a plant to survive disease. See *Immunity, Tolerance*.

REVERSION. Tendency of some cultivated plants to revert to what are considered ancestral characteristics.

ROGUING. Culling out of undesirable, inferior or off-type plants.

ROOT HARDY. Term applied to plant

that can survive mild-climate winters without damage, but suffers the loss of its aboveground growth in more severe climates, although its roots survive.

SAPROPHYTE. Organism (such as a mushroom) that is usually lacking in chlorophyll and feeds on dead organic matter.

SCALD. Injury to plant foliage or fruit resulting from overexposure to hot sun.

SCALE INSECT. Sedentary tough-shelled sucking insect that feeds on plant juices.

SCLEROTIUM. Compact mass of fungus filaments that can enable some disease organisms to survive for many years in soil, plant refuse or seed. Size of mass can vary from microscopic to baseball-size.

SET. Undersized bulb (of onions, for instance) grown for use the following season as early planting.

SHEET COMPOSTING. Applying compost materials directly to the garden instead of using a compost pile.

SHORT-DAY PLANT. One that blooms in fall or winter, responding to the shortened daylight at that time of year. See also *Long-Day Plant, Photoperiodism.*

SILT. Soil with particles that are somewhere between those of sand and clay in size.

SOUR SOIL. Soil that has had much of its calcium leached out by rainwater, with a resultant increase in acidity, sometimes to the extent of becoming unfit for plants.

SPHAGNUM. Light inert moss that eventually decomposes into peat moss.

STAMEN. The pollen-producing male sex organ in a flower.

STARTER SOLUTION. Weak fertilizer solution applied to plants at time of transplanting.

STOMA. Pore-like opening in leaf or stem. The plural is *stomata.*

SUBSOIL. The soil underlying the topsoil used for cultivation, usually harder-packed and with less organic matter.

SUCKER. Secondary shoot such as that arising from an axillary bud of the tomato plant or from the base of the corn plant.

SYSTEMIC. Spreading throughout the entire plant body via the vascular system.

TANKAGE. Fertilizer consisting of the ground-up dried remains of slaughtered animals.

TAPROOT. The primary downward root of a plant from which smaller side roots grow laterally.

TENDER. Descriptive of a plant that cannot be expected to withstand the normal degree of winter cold in any given area.

TENDRILS. The slender, coiled, fingerlike organs developed by certain climbing plants to grasp vertical structures as the plant grows.

TILTH. Term used to describe the condition of a soil. "Good tilth" means it has the right mixture of moisture, sand, clay and soil conditioners for easy workability.

TOLERANCE. A partial or limited ability on the part of a plant to withstand the onslaughts of disease, adverse climatic conditions or insect infestation. See *Immunity.*

TOP-DRESSING. An application of fertilizer that is simply spread on the surface of the soil, as distinguished from that plowed or spaded in.

TRACE ELEMENT. Chemical nutrient normally required only in small amounts. Also called "minor element." See *Micronutrient.*

TRANSPIRATION. The loss of moisture through the stomata of a plant.

TRENCHING. Deep digging of the garden soil and mixing in of soil conditioners.

UMBEL. Inflorescence in which flowers arise from a common stalk forming a more or less flattened or rounded cluster similar to the spokes of an umbrella.

VARIETY. A group of closely-related plants below the level of species, all of which share certain characteristics. Usually developed by breeding or selection. See also *Cultivar*.

VASCULAR. Pertaining to water-conducting tissue in plants that carries nutrients up and down between roots and foliage. See also *Phloem* and *Xylem*.

VECTOR. An agent (usually insect or animal) that transmits, carries or spreads disease.

VEGETATIVE GROWTH. Term applied to the growth of stems and foliage of plants, as opposed to flower and fruit.

VEGETATIVE PROPAGATION. Use of such methods as cuttings, grafts, layering, etc., to produce new plants rather than planting seed.

VERMICULITE. A lightweight rooting medium or soil additive made of expanded mica.

VIRUS. Type of pathogenic organism too small to be seen with a compound microscope.

WEATHER. Meteorological events — rain, heat, cold, wind — that in the aggregate over a long period of time constitute the *climate* of a particular region.

WETTING AGENT. Material included in spray solutions that breaks surface tension. This helps it to completely cover the surface area rather than merely adhering in scattered droplets.

WILTING. Drooping of leaves and stems, usually caused by a lack of water. Can also result from too much water, causing waterlogging, or damage to the plant's water-conducting system by disease or injury.

XYLEM. Tissue in plants through which water is conveyed up the stem from the roots. See also *Phloem* and *Vascular*.

SELECTED BIBLIOGRAPHY

Ingenious Kingdom: The Remarkable World of Plants. Henry and Rebecca Northen. Prentice-Hall, Inc. 1970.

Roots: Miracles Below. Charles Morrow Wilson. Doubleday, 1968.

Fundamentals of Horticulture. J. B. Edmond, A. M. Musser, F. S. Andrews. McGraw-Hill Book Co., Inc. 1957.

How To Grow Your Own Vegetables. Michael Kressy. Meredith Corp. 1973.

Sunset Guide to Organic Gardening. Editors of Sunset Books and Sunset Magazine. Lane Books, Menlo Park, Calif. 1971.

Herbs: How to grow them and how to use them. Helen Noyes Webster. Charles T. Branford Company, 1959.

Herbs. H. L. V. Fletcher. Drake Publishers, Inc. 1972.

Herbs for Every Garden. Gertrude B. Foster. E. P. Dutton & Co., Inc. 1966.

Illustrated Book of Garden Pests and Diseases. Edited by T. H. Everett. Greystone Press, N. Y.

All About Vegetables. Chevron Chemical Co. 1973.

The World in Your Garden. Camp - Boswell - Magness. National Geographic Society, Washington, D.C.

After a Hundred Years; The Yearbook of Agriculture, 1962. U.S. Dept. of Agriculture, Washington, D.C.

The Language of Gardening. George F. Hull. World Publishing Co., Cleveland and New York 1967.

Vegetable Crops. Thompson and Kelly. McGraw-Hill Book Company 1959.

The Buying Guide. Blue Goose, Inc. 1974.

Composition of Foods (Agriculture Handbook No. 8). U. S. Dept. of Agriculture, Washington, D.C.

Vegetable Gardening. Lane Publishing Co. 1975.

Food; The Yearbook of Agriculture 1959. U. S. Dept. of Agriculture, Washington, D.C.

Introduction to Nutrition. Henrietta Fleck, Ph.D. The Macmillan Company 1971.

The Vegetable Encyclopedia and Gardener's Guide. Victor A. Tiedjens, Ph.D. Garden City Publishing Co.

INDEX

(Bold face indicates main listing. Also see Glossary, p. 133.)